"The barn's on fire!" Rory Watson cried, clutching at the wooden five-bar gate.

Sarah peered past the dark house and saw that there was certainly something strange about the wooden barn. Its blackened boards were warped and cracked and through the gaps there was certainly a glow. But that glow wasn't flickering. It was steady. *"Someone inside has a light on,"* the girl told her brother. *"Let's go home."*

It was as Sarah turned away that she heard the sound. At first she thought it was an airplane taking off from a nearby airport. It had that whining, hissing tone. She looked up into the sky. Then the sound became more human—a wail of pain or a cry of anger . . .

THESE PUFFIN BOOKS WILL
REALLY CHILL YOU!

TRUE
GHOST STORIES

Terry Deary
Illustrated by David Wyatt

PUFFIN BOOKS

PUFFIN BOOKS
Published by the Penguin Group
Penguin Books USA Inc., 375 Hudson Street, New York, New York 10014, U.S.A.
Penguin Books Ltd, 27 Wrights Lane, London W8 5TZ, England
Penguin Books Australia Ltd, Ringwood, Victoria, Australia
Penguin Books Canada Ltd, 10 Alcorn Avenue, Toronto, Ontario, Canada M4V 3B2
Penguin Books (N.Z.) Ltd, 182-190 Wairau Road, Auckland 10, New Zealand

Penguin Books Ltd, Registered Offices: Harmondsworth, Middlesex, England

First published in Great Britain by Scholastic Ltd., 1995
Published in Puffin Books, 1996

1 3 5 7 9 10 8 6 4 2

Text copyright © Terry Deary, 1995
Illustrations copyright © David Wyatt, 1995
All rights reserved

LIBRARY OF CONGRESS CATALOGING-IN-PUBLICATION DATA

Deary, Terry.
True ghost stories / Terry Deary ; illustrated by David Wyatt.
p. cm.
Summary: A collection of ghost stories from around the world based on experiences
which someone has claimed are factual.
ISBN 0-14-038224-0 (pbk.)
1. Ghosts—Juvenile literature. [1. Ghosts.] I. Wyatt, David, ill. II. Title.
BF1461.D42 1996 133.1—dc20 96-20241 CIP AC

Printed in the United States of America

Contents

INTRODUCTION

Do you believe in ghosts?

- Is there something outside the natural life . . . a *super-natural* life?
- Do people have spirits as well as bodies?
- Do those spirits survive the deaths of the bodies?
- And if the spirits survive, do they go on to another life? . . . an *after*-life?
- Or do some come back to our world?
- And, if they do come back, can some living people see them?

These are the questions that interest most people. This book will try to answer them honestly by presenting some of the most fascinating cases. The cases are retold as "stories" to entertain you . . . and maybe send some shivers down your spine. But the book then gives some fascinating facts about the stories to help you make up your own mind about the mysteries of the supernatural.

Do *I* believe in ghosts?

Let me tell you my own story. Let me tell you about Mara . . .

Durham, England – November 1993

Mara is a Great Dane dog. When we adopted her she was a poor, thin creature. She'd been badly treated as a puppy and rescued from her cruel owners just in time.

For the first year in our home she was timid and afraid of humans – too timid even to bark. But slowly she learned to trust us. It was a great day when a stranger came to the door and Mara let loose a window-rattling "Woof!"

But she's never really recovered from her bad treatment and her brain is slightly damaged. Sometimes she has a small fit and wakes up shivering and lost. It takes her half an hour to remember where she is.

In the winter of 1993 she was really ill. She raced around wildly and seemed desperate to be out of the house. Someone opened the door and she disappeared along the road.

We waited for her to return. She didn't. Perhaps she had run too far while her mind was disturbed. When she recovered she must have been truly lost.

Snow was lying on the ground that night. Mara hated the cold and loved sleeping in front of the fire whenever she could. A night sleeping out in that February cold could kill her. We reported her disappearance to the police and waited.

The next day there was a phone call. Someone had seen a large, dark grey dog on a farm five kilometres from our house. They told the police. The police told us. My daughter, Sara, and I jumped in the car and hurried to the farm.

It was five o'clock on a bitterly cold evening. The sun had set but the sky was a clear ice-blue and snow lay in a thin, crisp covering at the edge of the road. We turned off the main road and on to the farm track. The farm was two kilometres down the track, but halfway along was a small forest of fir trees that the road cut through.

Let me get the next part right, because it's important.

The farm track ran straight into the wood. I was 300 metres away from the spot where the road entered the wood. As I looked ahead a dog trotted across the road. It was a large, dark dog. I had no doubt that it was Mara.

"There she is!" I cried.

Sara had been looking out of the side window. "Where?" she said.

"She ran across the road and vanished into the wood," I explained.

Sara shrugged. She'd seen nothing. I hurried down the frozen rutted track to the place where I'd seen her and skidded to a halt. There was no dog in sight. But the woods were thick and you could soon have lost sight of an elephant in that undergrowth.

We called her name. Nothing. Then we looked down at the snowy verges. There were the huge paw-prints of our dog.

The tracks seemed to disappear into the wood, but there was a wire fence around the edge and we couldn't follow. After half an hour of following tracks in the snow we climbed back into the car and drove on to the farm. Yes, they'd seen the dog, but that was two or three hours ago. They'd called for her but she'd run away.

We went back to the woods where I'd seen her. It was growing too dark now to see anything. We went home.

As we walked through the front door Mara trotted out to greet us, wagging her tail. At five o'clock she had wandered into the garden of a friend at the far side of the village and been given a lift home, but at ten-past five I'd seen her quite clearly trotting across the road five kilometres away . . . or had I seen her "ghost"?

Could a dog be in two places at once? That's impossible. I *hadn't* seen her. So what *had* I seen?

A "double", a ghost-hunter would tell you. An "apparition".

There are two kinds of apparition – ones inside your head and ones outside. No one else saw Mara at the time I did, so it was probably *all in my mind*. I desperately *wanted* to find her there – as I drove to the farm I could almost picture my first sight of her. I simply saw *what I wanted to see*.

But to this day I would swear I *didn't* imagine it. I'm sure that I saw *something* that looked like our dog. If I didn't imagine it, then I saw a ghostly apparition.

It's an amazing fact that there are more reports of apparitions of the *living* than the *dead*! Some say a disturbed mind (as Mara's is) can throw out images of itself where a sound mind is too much in control.

So, yes, I believe in apparitions. People who have seen a ghost tend to believe in them. People who haven't seen one have to rely on reported stories and decide if they are true. That's what this book will try to help you do.

THE HALLOWE'EN GHOST
The Restless Mummy

Manchester, 1990

"The barn's on fire!" Rory Watson cried, clutching at the wooden five-bar gate.

His sister sighed. She knew it was a mistake to bring Rory out on Hallowe'en, but Mum had insisted, "Take Rory with you, Sarah."

"He gets so excited, Mum. He's embarrassing," Sarah had complained.

"Take him or you don't go," her mother had said firmly. "There are two turnips on the table. Start hollowing them out."

And Sarah had been right. Rory had thrown himself into the trick-or-treat visits as if he really believed he were a ghost. He'd scared the old lady in Osborne Terrace half out of her wits. She'd threatened to call the police.

Now they were on their way home. They had to pass old Birchen Farm. Sarah didn't really believe in ghosts but the place gave her the creeps even in the daytime. Over the years a housing estate had grown up around the farm. Its fields were covered by rows of houses and roads and paths. Now the farmhouse and the barn had only a small paddock with a few grimy sheep.

"It *is*, Sarah! The barn's on *fire!*" Rory insisted.

She sighed again and walked back to where he stood. Sarah peered past the dark house and saw that there was certainly something strange about the wooden barn. Its blackened boards were warped and cracked and through the gaps there was certainly a glow. But that glow wasn't flickering. It was steady. "Someone inside has a light on," the girl told her brother. "Let's go home."

It was as Sarah turned away that she heard the sound. At

first she thought it was an aeroplane taking off from nearby Manchester Airport. It had that whining, hissing tone. She looked up into the sky. Then the sound became more human – a wail of pain or a cry of anger. The girl reached for Rory's arm but he was moving so quickly that she missed. He tumbled past her and sped down the road. Sarah stretched her long legs to catch him. Something banged painfully at her knee. It was the turnip lantern. She threw it in the gutter and sprinted home.

Brother and sister fell through the kitchen door together and it was five minutes before their mother could get the story from them clearly.

She nodded as she sat at the kitchen table. "Yes. There is a story about that farm."

"Tell us, Mum," Sarah said.

Mrs Watson looked at her son doubtfully. Sarah was right. Rory was excitable. "There's a football match on the television, Rory. Why don't you go and watch it with your dad?"

"Okay," the boy said, picking up a can of soft drink and hurrying off to the living room.

"So, what's the story?" Sarah asked.

"Your gran told it to me. She was just a girl when the old mansion, Birchen Bower, was knocked down. She can still remember it. But the story goes back even further. It goes back to the 1740s when a lady called Miss Hannah Beswick lived there. It seems she was a bit of a miser."

"Like Mr Scrooge in the Christmas story," Sarah put in.

"That's right. Miss Beswick was so mean she wouldn't pay someone to manage the farm; she did it all herself until she became too old. They say she made a fortune."

"What did she do with it?"

"In 1745 a Scottish army invaded England. When Miss Beswick heard they were as far south as Manchester she did what a lot of rich people did. She hid her treasures."

Sarah's eyes lit up. "Treasure? What sort of treasure?"

"Mostly silver and gold. She hid it somewhere near Birchen Bower mansion, but she worked alone and no one knew where it was."

"So how do you know it was silver and gold? Did the Scottish soldiers find it?" her daughter asked.

"I'm coming to that," Mrs Watson said. "The Scots never came to Manchester and they were defeated. The war was soon over, but Miss Beswick decided not to disturb her treasure. There were more villains around than Scottish soldiers. She might have lived and died in

16

peace but something shocking happened that changed her life, something so horrible that I wouldn't tell Rory; you know he sometimes has nightmares."

Sarah nodded and looked towards the living room. The door was closed. Her mother lowered her voice. "Miss Beswick's brother, John, fell ill. The doctor went to his house and declared him dead. He was laid in his coffin and Miss Beswick went to pay her last respects."

"What does that mean?" the girl asked.

"She went to have a last look at her brother in his coffin before they buried him."

The girl shuddered and wrapped two hands around her mug of hot chocolate. "That's horrible."

Mrs Watson shrugged. "It shows respect to the dead," she explained. "Anyway, Miss Beswick said goodbye to her brother and the undertaker moved in to put the lid on the coffin and screw it down. But just as she turned away she thought she saw the cheek twitch ever so slightly. She called for a mirror and held it under her brother's nose. It was soon covered with a faint mist. He was breathing!"

"They were going to bury him alive!" Sarah gasped.

"They were. The doctor was called and the 'dead' man was revived. In fact they say he went on to live many more healthy years. But the effect on Miss Beswick was shattering. From then on the old woman had a terror of being buried alive. So she made a curious addition to her will."

"She asked not to be buried for a week or two after she died, I suppose," Sarah said thoughtfully. "That's what I'd do."

Her mother gave a faint smile. "Miss Beswick went one better. She asked to be buried . . . never!"

"That's impossible! She'd go mouldy!" Sarah cried, pulling a disgusted face.

Mrs Watson leaned across the table. "Would she? I thought you were studying the Ancient Egyptians at school this term."

"We are, but . . . but . . . they turned their kings into mummies!"

"Exactly!"

The girl's mouth dropped open. "Miss Beswick asked to be turned into a mummy?"

"Yes. She left money to the family doctor, Doctor White, and to all his descendants on the condition that her body was never placed below the ground. Stranger still, she insisted that her body should be brought back to Birchen Bower once every twenty-one years. And then she died."

"And Doctor White turned her into a mummy?"

"Miss Beswick died so suddenly that her great fortune of hidden treasure wasn't found. But the doctor wrapped the corpse in bandages, leaving only the face exposed, then treated it with tar to preserve it."

"Is this true?" the girl asked suddenly.

"Oh, yes. The body was put on display at Manchester Natural History Museum and lots of people saw it. It was there for over a hundred years. And five times the body was taken back to the old farm. They placed it in the barn."

"In the barn where we saw the light tonight? That's disgusting!" Sarah said.

"In 1868 the museum thought that too. They had Miss Beswick buried in a proper cemetery," her mother explained.

"I thought you said Gran told you this story. Even Gran isn't old enough to remember things from a hundred years ago," Sarah said suddenly.

Mrs Watson grinned. "No, she's not quite that old. But just because Miss Beswick was buried doesn't mean that's an end to the story. You see, she never really left Birchen Bower. The huge mansion was divided into flats. Several families lived there and most of them reported meeting old Miss Beswick's ghost at some time. First there was the rustle of her silk dress, then her figure, dressed in black, glided into the kitchen. She always disappeared at the same flagstone in the floor."

"What was so special about it?" Sarah asked.

Mrs Watson shrugged. "We'll never know. They pulled the old house down. But the barn's still there, and that's where Gran comes into the story. It seems she met a rich man once who told her the story of The Mummy at Birchen Bower. He then said he'd been walking past the barn one Hallowe'en when he saw a glowing light coming from inside. He thought it was on fire, but when he went to investigate the light went out and there was nothing in the barn. He was an inquisitive man, though, and he asked the people in the area what they knew about the old barn. He pieced together the story of Miss Beswick and came up with a curious idea."

Sarah nodded. "The ghost of the old woman was wandering around the barn. But why?"

"That's what the rich man worked out. When would Miss Beswick have wandered around the barn, with a glowing lantern, when she was alive?"

The girl frowned and concentrated. "When . . . when she was hiding her treasure?" Her face cleared. "She hid her treasure in the barn!"

Mrs Watson gave her daughter a playful pat on the head. "Well done, Sherlock! The man went back to the barn and started digging. He found several gold pieces and that's what made him rich. That was back in the 1920s when Gran was just a little girl."

"So why did we see that light again tonight?" Sarah asked.

"Ah, it seems that the theft of the gold just infuriated the ghost. One of Gran's friends was walking past the barn one night and saw the ghost of Miss Beswick again. The old woman was wearing her black dress with a white collar. The figure was making terrible wailing sounds and shaking her fist as if she was upset."

"That would be the wailing I heard!" Sarah said.

"Perhaps, perhaps. Or maybe it was just a jet aircraft from the airport. You don't want to get too scared; you probably just made a mistake."

"But the light?" Sarah said.

"Maybe someone was working in the barn."

The girl nodded and finished her cup of hot chocolate. She stretched. "I think I'll go to bed."

"Sweet dreams," her mother smiled.

"Yes . . . it was just the sound of a jet. And the story's just some old ghost story. It's not as if I *saw* a ghost, is it?" she said.

"That's right," Mrs Watson agreed. "Just don't tell Rory the story. He's not as level-headed as you."

"I won't, Mum. Goodnight."

"Goodnight!"

Sarah was surprised when Rory insisted on walking past Birchen Farm on the way to school the next day.

"You're not scared, then?" the girl asked him carefully.

"Scared? No!" the boy said.

"You ran fast enough last night."

Rory nodded and turned a little red. "You scared me when you started screaming," he said.

"You ran before I yelled," she said.

Rory stopped and frowned. "I did?"

"Yes. As soon as you heard the sound."

Her brother looked at her with wide and wondering eyes. "Sound? I didn't hear a sound."

"The screaming of that jet. It scared me. That's what

must have scared you, dummy!"

"Oh, no," the boy said seriously. "It was that woman that scared me."

It was Sarah's turn to be puzzled. "What woman?"

"The one in the black dress – a long black dress with a white collar. She gave me a real fright!"

"Because you thought she was a ghost?" Sarah asked.

"No! There's no such things as ghosts! It was because she was coming towards us looking very angry and shaking her fist. Maybe she was fed up with kids going trick-or-treating at her door, eh, Sarah?"

"Maybe," the girl said faintly.

"Come on," Rory tugged at her sleeve. "We'll be late for school."

"There are worse things that can happen," Sarah said quietly, looking at the dark and gloomy barn.

"Such as what?"

"Such as being buried alive."

"Hah!" the boy laughed and began to run down the street. "And Mum says *I've* got a strong imagination!"

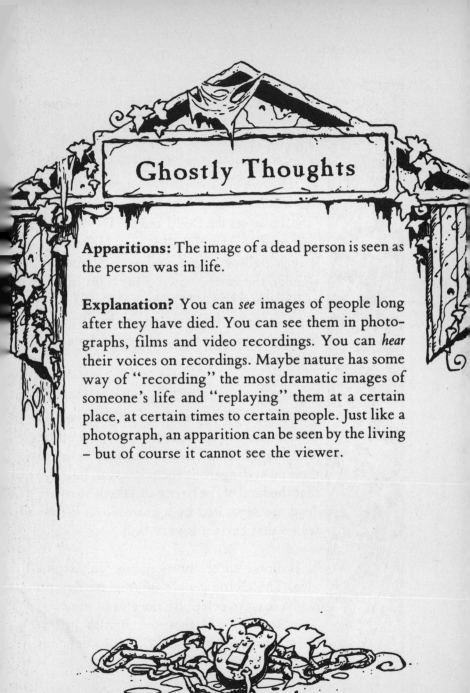

Ghostly Thoughts

Apparitions: The image of a dead person is seen as the person was in life.

Explanation? You can *see* images of people long after they have died. You can see them in photographs, films and video recordings. You can *hear* their voices on recordings. Maybe nature has some way of "recording" the most dramatic images of someone's life and "replaying" them at a certain place, at certain times to certain people. Just like a photograph, an apparition can be seen by the living – but of course it cannot see the viewer.

Hallowe'en – FACT FILE

Did you know . . .?

1. Hallowe'en lanterns are a reminder of an old legend concerning an Irishman called Jack. He upset the Devil and the Devil threw a piece of coal from Hell at him. Jack caught it in a hollow turnip and was doomed to wander the earth showing his light till the end of time. Jack-o'-Lantern still makes his appearance at Hallowe'en in the shape of turnip lanterns which are carved out by children.

2. Hallowe'en is known as All Souls' Night – the time of the year when the ghosts of the dead are said to roam about. It is also a time when witches and devils are said to be at their most dangerous and powerful. Imagine that the land of the living and the land of the dead are separated by a curtain. At Hallowe'en that curtain is very thin.

3. Hallowe'en celebrations are an ancient idea. The Celtic people of Ancient Britain held a feast to celebrate the end of summer. The Romans said that the British priests (Druids) made human sacrifices to the gods at the celebration. They claimed the sacri-

fices were made by fastening prisoners in a huge wooden cage and setting fire to it. (The Romans were probably lying.)

4. The Romans celebrated a day of the dead on 21 February but Pope Boniface changed it to All Saints' Day and made it 13 May. A later Pope, Gregory III, changed it again to 1 November. The "eve" of 1 November is, of course, 31 October, and that's when most people celebrate "All Hallows' Eve" (or Hallowe'en) now.

5. On Hallowe'en many children enjoy dressing up and pretending to be ghosts who have slipped through the "curtain" from the

world of the dead. They then call at houses and threaten the owners with a haunting if they aren't given a gift – this is called "trick or treat" in the United States. But a Chinese woman who moved to Britain had never heard of Hallowe'en or the game. She really believed there was a ghost at her door and she threw a pan of boiling water over the eight-year-old boy. Only his mask and bin-liner costume saved him from serious injury. The poor woman was ordered to pay the boy £750 for the scalds he received. Some trick – some treat!

GHOSTS AT WORK
The Phantom Boots

Say the word "ghost" and what do most people think of? A haunted castle or a creepy house? The spirit of a great and famous person? But there's no reason why ghosts should have to live in those draughty miserable places. They can appear in the least likely spots at the most peculiar times.

This story was told by a coal miner, John Kitchin, and he swears it's true . . .

Scotland, 1973

I once knew a night-shift engineer. Sid, his name was. What his second name was I can't quite remember.

He worked up in the main control room of the pit. He used to dress like that cartoon boy, Dennis the Menace, even though he was fifty years old, and he had this big spiky haircut, straight across the top.

He was in the control room one night, looking after tub-loading, from eleven o'clock at night till seven in the morning.

It's bright up in the control room – better than the filth and dust below the ground. Still, the night shift hours can drag a bit when you're up there all on your own.

Then, in the middle of the night, around three o'clock, he gets a phone call from below the ground; I think it may have come from Number 4 transfer point, somewhere about a mile from the pit-head where two roadways meet underground.

The main conveyor pulls the coal from out the pit. It's the transfer point lad that's on the phone.

Sid says, "What can I do for you, Tony lad?"

"You'll have to stop these belts and get some other feller on my job," the young lad says. "'Cos I'm not moving from this refuge hole!"

The refuge hole is the lad's control box where he watches the coal run down the big conveyor belts.

Sid says, "Well, you know we can't stop the belts. What's the matter with you, Tony lad?"

He says, "There's a pair of boots that's dancing on the belt!"

Now, Sid being Sid, he says, "All right, lad, you've had your little joke. There's no way we can stop that belt."

"You've got to stop the belt and then you've got to get somebody else down here, 'cos I'm not moving from this refuge hole," he says.

So Sid says, "Do you know what that means? What stopping the belt means in terms of lost production?"

He says, "I don't care what it means, 'cos I'm not moving from this hole. And there's a great big pair of boots that's dancing on the belt, I'm telling you."

"Lad," Sid says, "I've been around for fifty years, and I think you've pulled my old leg long enough. There's no way I'm switching off that belt."

Young Tony says, "You'd better stop the belt and then you'd better get somebody down here, 'cos I'm telling you that there's a pair of boots that's dancing on the belt."

The argument goes on for about ten minutes. Finally Sid says, "You just sit down, Tony son, and think about it."

"I've thought about it long enough. I'm staying in this hole until you stop the pair of boots that's dancing on the belt."

Now Sidney thinks, a joke's a joke, but this joke's just gone far enough! The old chap starts to lose his head. "Do you know what you're going to get if you don't stop this stupid game? You're going to get the sack, young man."

The lad says, "I don't care what I get. Just stop the belt and get somebody down there."

Now, if there's a stoppage you have to put the reason, don't you? You have to write that reason in the log book. And Sid hates to write reports. So Sid says, "Right, I've had enough of you. I'm going to call the manager."

"Call who you like," the lad says. "Stop the belt and get somebody down here, 'cos I'm scared."

Sid calls the manager and *he* speaks down on the phone to Tony. "Now then, Tony lad, we'll leave the belt running but we'll send two men down there to have a look. We'll send a man down 'A' shaft and we'll send a man down 'B' shaft. They'll be sure to get these . . . boots."

"That's not good enough! You've got to stop the rotten belt!" the lad sobs.

"We've been in touch with the two deputies. They're coming now, they won't be long," the manager says.

"Are you going to stop the belt?" the lad cries, and he's screaming now.

So the belt is stopped.

That is all the coal work in the mine stopped. The pit can shift six hundred tons of coal in every hour.

The pit goes silent as a graveyard. Time passes as Deputy A and Deputy B walk slowly down the passages to the transfer point. And then, back in Sid's control room, there comes a crackle on the radio.

Deputy A cries, "Right, we've got him! Some bloke climbing on the belt."

A click and Deputy B comes in, "Yes, I can see him. Now we've got him."

Then silence once again. And then a sudden cry. "He's gone!" one of the men cries. "He must have run past you."

"There's no one gone past me," the other says.

"In that case there's just one place he can be. He must have run along that passageway between us."

"Hah!" the first one laughs. "That passageway is blind. There's no way out."

Sid nods to the manager. "They'll catch him now. He's headed down a dead-end passage. Now he's had it. Now we'll see who's playing silly jokes and trying to scare poor Tony there."

"He's for the sack," the manager says sternly.

"What, the lad?"

"No," the manager says. "This bloke that's playing games. He must have cost the pit a thousand pounds already." He taps his fingers on the table top and waits for the radio call. "Come on, come on," he mutters, staring at the radio. "How long is that passage anyway?" he asks.

"It's only short," Sid says. "They must have caught him up by now."

"Then why have they not called us back?"

"Perhaps the feller had a struggle. If they're too busy wrestling with him they can't make a radio call," Sid explains.

It seemed an age before the call came through. Deputy B is almost whispering in the microphone. "There's no one here," he says. His voice is shaking.

"There has to be," old Sid says.

"There's not!" the other deputy cuts in. "It's like he walked into a wall of coal. He never came past me."

"And he never came past me," his mate agrees. "It's dark down here but the passageway is narrow. No one could have run back past us."

"Come back up," the manager says, "and bring young Tony with you."

Half an hour later Tony is sitting in Sid's control room, drinking hot sweet tea.

"I saw the boots!" he says. His face is smudged with coal but that can't hide the grey shade to his skin.

"I might have said that you imagined it . . ." the manager begins.

"But we both saw it too," Deputy A says and he shakes his head. He's worked there longer than old Sid himself. He thought that he'd seen everything there was to see.

"Dancing on the belt," his mate agrees.

"You know the men who work down there," the manager says. "So tell me who it was."

"I couldn't see him very clearly, understand. Just those dusty boots that were dancing on the belt. His head was bent down so it wouldn't touch the roof. I only saw the black cloth cap."

"Cloth cap!" old Sid says. "No one wears cloth caps these days. Not for fifty years or more. They all wear helmets underground."

The man shrugs, "Aye, you're right . . . but this man wore a black cloth cap."

No one cares to argue with the man.

The manager looks down at Tony. The boy has stopped his shaking now but still his pale eyes stare down at the floor. Maybe he's seeing something deep below the ground. "Only the boots," he muttered. "If I'd seen the feller I wouldn't have been so scared. But all I saw were the boots. Dancing. Dancing on the belt like they were happy."

"Maybe his head and shoulders were up in the shadows," the deputy says, quite gentle.

"That's right," his mate agreed. "We saw the whole man . . . both of us."

The lad looks up quite sharp, his eyes as wild as my Uncle Paddy's terrier. "I know what I saw. And I didn't see a man. I saw a pair of boots as clear as I can see you now. I'm not going mad, you know. I'm not, you know. I saw them."

The manager just nods and mutters, "You get off home now, Tony lad. We'll see you back tomorrow night."

The boy stands up, puts the empty cup down and trudges out of the control room.

"There'll have to be a report," Sid says. "We've lost a thousand tons of coal, stopping the conveyor belts like that."

"Yes. Yes," the manager says. "You write up a report."

"Aye, but what do I say?" Sid asks sharply.

The manager turns his collar up and stares out into the early morning dark. "You'll think of something," he says.

"I'll think of *something*," Sid says, angry now. "But can I think of *something* so I won't look *stupid*? I can't go and write those things about a pair of old boots dancing on the belt, can I, sir? Now, can I?"

The manager steps out into the cold and doesn't give an answer.

Then Deputy A rubs a grimy hand over his grey hair. "Young Tony must have had a fright," he says.

"We'll not see that young man again," Sid says.

And Sid was right. The boy went home and never turned up at the pit again.

A few years later old Sid left the pit himself. Only then did he tell the story of the boots – the boots that danced along the belt and cost a thousand tons of coal.

A funny chap, old Sid.

Pair of braces like Dennis the Menace. Big spiky haircut, straight across the top.

Tough as a pit pony, old Sid. But he's still haunted by a pair of boots.

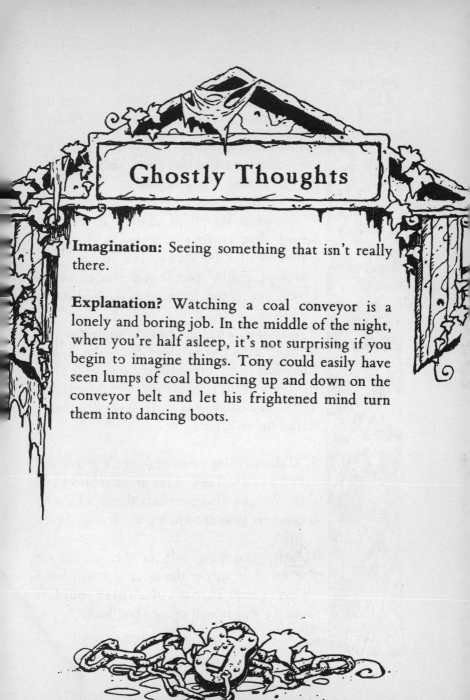

Ghostly Thoughts

Imagination: Seeing something that isn't really there.

Explanation? Watching a coal conveyor is a lonely and boring job. In the middle of the night, when you're half asleep, it's not surprising if you begin to imagine things. Tony could easily have seen lumps of coal bouncing up and down on the conveyor belt and let his frightened mind turn them into dancing boots.

Charms Against Ghosts – FACT FILE

For thousands of years people have feared ghosts and have made up weird spells and charms to defend against the dead. These include:

1. **Brooms**. People of Eastern Europe believed that putting a broom under your pillow would keep away evil spirits while you slept. English people preferred to lay the broom across the doorstep of the house.

2. **Candles**. The light from a candle was said to keep evil spirits away from the dying. They had to be left burning for a week after the death of the person to protect their spirit. The Irish custom was to circle the dead body with twelve candles.

3. **Cairns**. Piles of stones over a grave are called a cairn. They deter grave robbers and their weight also prevents the dead rising from their graves to haunt the living.

4. **Salt**. Carrying salt in the pocket or scattering it across the doorstep will keep ghosts at bay. Throw a pinch over your left shoulder and it will bring good luck.

5. **Iron**. Iron is a powerful defence against ghosts, witches and other evil spirits. An iron horse-shoe hung on a stable door will protect a house or stable. More gruesome, iron nails taken from a coffin will stop you having nightmares if you drive them into your bedroom door. An iron bar left lying across a grave will stop a ghost rising.

6. **Silver**. Most people know the legend that only silver bullets can kill vampires. This metal is also a defence against ghosts, especially if made into the shape of a cross.

7. **Crosses**. If someone is surprised by a ghost then making the sign of the cross in the air will protect him/her against evil.

8. **Prayers**. Christians believe that saying the Lord's Prayer will protect them against ghosts. They also believe that saying the same prayer *backwards* is a way of raising the Devil. A common test for a witch was to ask him or her to say the Lord's Prayer. A witch (a servant of the Devil) would not be able to do it, and would be punished for even one mistake. The accused witch would be very nervous; it would be easy to make a mistake while you were so frightened. So the test was hardly a fair one.

GHOSTLY CURSES
The Flying Dutchman

Some ghosts are said to wander the earth as a punishment for offending a god or a devil. They are cursed, and so are the people they meet. These ghosts don't only appear on land. The most famous sea ghost is probably the Flying Dutchman.

July 1881, Australian coast

George was cold. He paced up and down the deck of the warship to keep warm. He was only sixteen and the youngest sailor aboard *HMS Inconstant*. That was why they gave him the worst job. Being on night watch in the winter seas was uncomfortable . . . and boring.

The ship churned through the icy sea and towards the setting moon. Two or three more hours of darkness, the cadet thought. At least in the daylight he'd be able to see the Australian coast. That would be something to look at, something to break the monotony of deep purple sky and darker sea.

George stared at the ribbon of moonlight shimmering on the sea in front of him. When the ship appeared ahead of him it took a while for him to react. It was so sudden and unexpected. It seemed to have grown from melted moonlight. The wind from the Antarctic stung his eyes as he squinted into it. At the same moment a voice called down from the lookout post at the top of the mast, "Ship ahead!"

It was a sailing ship in full sail, racing over the water. It would cut across the course of *HMS Inconstant* at any moment. The laws of the sea said that the sailing ship had the right of way. George began to run towards the bridge where the First Mate was in control. "Ship ahead, Sir! Off the starboard bow."

"A little late with that sighting, Sir," the First Mate said sourly. "I saw it before you came in."

"Sorry, Sir, it just appeared."

The senior officer gave a brief nod and signalled to the engine room to slow down. He stared through the window at the glowing shape of the sailing ship and frowned.

"It's all wrong. No sailing ship ever sailed that quickly in a light breeze like this. It's all wrong," the officer said. He turned to a sailor alongside him. "Send a signal to that ship. She doesn't seem to have seen us."

"Yes, Sir," the sailor answered and turned on the powerful lamp. He began tapping out an urgent signal but there was no reply from the strange sailing ship.

Other officers of the watch gathered on the bridge to see what would happen next. The sailing ship passed across the bows of *HMS Inconstant* and out of the light of the moon. As it sailed away from the warship it seemed to fade. Within a minute the ocean was as empty and calm as ever. The First Mate took a telescope and scanned the sea. He lowered it at last and shook his head.

"*The Flying Dutchman*," he said. Some of the older sailors nodded and one or two looked afraid. "Back to your duties," the First Mate snapped and the crew hurried to obey him.

George climbed back to the upper deck and stood next to a midshipman. "What did he mean?" the cadet asked.

"It was a ghost ship, Sir," the midshipman said. "And they do say that anyone who sees her is cursed."

"I've heard about ghost ships, of course. What's the story of this *Flying Dutchman*?"

"Well, Sir, many years ago there was a ship's captain who feared neither God nor his saints. He is said to have been a Dutchman, but I do not know, and it doesn't really matter what town he came from.

"He once set off on a voyage south. All went well until he came near land. He used to boast that no storm, however terrible, could make him turn back.

"On this voyage south he reached the Cape of Good Hope when he ran into a head-wind that would have blown the horns off an ox. Between the wind and the huge waves his ship was in deadly danger. 'Captain,' the crew pleaded, 'we are lost if you don't turn back. We shall sink if you try to go round the Cape in this wind. We are all doomed and there isn't even a priest on board to bless us before we die. We are surely bound for hell!'

"The captain laughed at the fears of his passengers and crew. Instead of listening to them he started singing. The songs were so ungodly that they could have drawn thunderbolts from heaven just by themselves.

"Then the captain called for his pipe and his tankard of

beer. He smoked and drank as happily as if he were in the tavern back home.

"The others pleaded again with him to turn back. The more they pleaded the more stubborn he became.

"The storm snapped the masts and tore the sails away. Captain van der Decken laughed and jeered at the terrified passengers.

"The storm grew more and more violent but the captain ignored it just as he ignored the people on his ship. When the men tried to force him to take shelter in a bay by grabbing the wheel he snatched their leader and threw him overboard.

"As he did this the clouds parted and a shape appeared on the deck in front of him. The shape may have been God himself; if not, it was certainly sent by Him. The crew and the passengers were speechless with terror. The captain went on smoking his pipe. He didn't even take his cap off in the presence of the Almighty.

"The Shape spoke. 'Captain, you are a stubborn man.'

"'And you are a villain! Who wants a nice, smooth voyage? Not I! I want nothing from you, so clear off unless you want me to blow your brains out.'

"The Shape shrugged its shoulders and didn't answer.

"The captain grabbed a pistol, pulled back the hammer and pressed the trigger. But the bullet didn't reach the Shape; it turned around and went through van der Decken's hand. At this his temper exploded and he jumped up to strike the Shape in the face. But as he raised his arm it fell limp and paralysed by his side. He cursed and called the Shape all the evil names under the sun.

"At this the Shape spoke again. 'From this moment on you are cursed. You are sentenced to sail forever without rest, without anchorage, without reaching a port of any kind. You shall never taste beer or tobacco again. Your drink shall be bitter water and your meat shall be red hot iron. Only a cabin boy will remain of all your crew. Horns will grow from his forehead and he will have a tiger's face and skin rougher than a dogfish.'

"Captain van der Decken realized his stupidity and groaned. The Shape went on, 'You will always be on duty and you will never be able to sleep, no matter how much you long for it. The moment you close your eyes a sword will pierce your body. And, since you like tormenting sailors, you shall torment them till the end of time.'

"The captain smiled at the thought. The Shape said to him. 'You shall become the evil spirit of the sea. You will travel all oceans without stopping or resting. Your ship will bring bad luck to all who see it.'

"'I'll drink to that!' the captain laughed.

"'And on the Day of Judgement, the Devil shall claim your soul.'

"'I don't give a fig for the Devil!' he replied.

"The Shape vanished and the captain found himself alone with the cabin boy, who had already been changed into the evil creature that the Shape had described. The rest of the crew had vanished.

"From that day to this the Flying Dutchman has sailed the seven seas and takes pleasure in tricking unlucky sailors. He sets ships on wrong routes, leads them into rocks and wrecks them. He turns their wine sour and all their food to beans.

"The Flying Dutchman can change the appearance of his ship whenever he wants and, through the years, he has collected a new crew. All of them are the worst bullies and

pirates ever to sail the seas. Every one of them is cursed and doomed like the Flying Dutchman himself."

"Thanks," the young cadet said. "It was an interesting story. But you don't believe that stuff about a curse, do you?"

"We'll see, sir," the midshipman said. "We'll see."

HMS Inconstant sailed on over the smooth sea and at daybreak George went down to his cabin. He opened his diary and began to write:

At 4 a.m. the Flying Dutchman *crossed our bows. She gave off a strange phosphorescent light like a phantom ship all aglow; in the middle of the glow her masts, spars and sails stood out in silhouette as she came up on the port bow where an officer of the watch also saw her as did a midshipman who was sent forward. But when he arrived at the bows there was no trace or sign whatever of any ship, near or on the horizon, the night being clear and the sea calm.*

As the cadet finished writing there was a tap on his cabin door. "Breakfast, Your Highness."

Prince George yawned, stretched and rose to his feet. The young sailor later became King George V, but his meeting with the *Flying Dutchman* was an experience that stayed in his memory for the rest of his eventful life.

Ghostly Thoughts

Demons: Evil spirits that try to interfere with human life. They can take many forms – lights, sounds or voices inside a victim's head, fairies, goblins, phantom animals, or phantom ships like the *Flying Dutchman*. They often enter a human body and possess it; that person then becomes a "witch" and performs evil deeds for the demon.

Explanation? Some religions believe that pure goodness is their "God", but pure evil can also exist in a spirit form as a demon. You may choose to believe that. The superstitious used to say that the only way to get rid of the demon was to destroy the body it lived in – that's why they burned witches. Nowadays we aren't so cruel or stupid.

The story of the Flying Dutchman *seems very unlikely yet some researchers claim the legend is based on fact.*

The Dutch captain's name was Hendrik van der Decken and he lived in the 1660s. Van der Decken was a greedy and ruthless ship's captain who set sail from Amsterdam to make his fortune in the East Indies. Over the years, countless sailors from around the world have sworn that they've seen something strange on the ocean. Can they all be wrong?

1. **The Dutchman's curse**. Prince George's sighting was backed up by thirteen sailors on his ship and on other ships that were sailing alongside her. If seeing the *Flying Dutchman* was unlucky then the curse worked for Prince George's ship, *HMS Inconstant*. Later that same day the seaman who'd first seen the ghost ship fell to his death from the mast. The admiral of the fleet died shortly afterwards.

2. **The *Lady Lovibond***. Britain has its own phantom ship. On 13 February 1748 the *Lady Lovibond* was sailing by the dangerous Goodwin Sands off the coast of Kent, England. Her captain, Simon Peel, was on honeymoon, with his bride and several

wedding guests. But a jealous sailor (who was also in love with the bride) killed Peel and steered the ship to disaster on the sands. On 13 February 1798, fifty years later to the day, a fishing boat spotted a ship of the *Lady Lovibond*'s description heading for the sands. The crew heard laughter and women's voices. It sounded as though a party was being held on board. But when the ship hit the sands it broke up and vanished. The same vision was seen in 1848 and 1898. Ghost-hunters were on the lookout in 1948 but saw nothing in the mist. Perhaps in 1998 it will be back . . .

3. **The blazing ghost ship**. America's *Flying Dutchman* is the *Palantine*. It arrived off the coast of Rhode Island packed with Dutch colonists in 1752. A storm drove it off course and washed the captain overboard. The ship was driven on to rocks and started to break up. Local fishermen rowed out and took the passengers to safety but began stripping the ship of its valuable cargo before it sank. To cover up their crime they set the ship ablaze, but as they rowed home they were horrified to see a woman come up on deck. She'd been hiding from the looters. Her screams carried across the water until the flames swallowed her. Over the centuries a blazing ship has been seen by many witnesses off the coast of New England.

4. **The ghost under the sea**. Not only ancient sailing ships are ghostly. The German submarine *UB65* was cursed from the start. Workmen building her had fatal accidents then, on her maiden voyage, an officer was killed in an explosion. From then on the ghost of the officer was seen on board. A new captain and crew were appointed who did not believe in ghosts and for a while the ghost did not appear. But when that captain left the submarine the ghost returned. One sailor went mad with fear and jumped overboard. Still the submarine survived enemy attacks until, near the end of the First World War, it mysteriously blew up, killing the entire crew. An accident? Or a ghost's revenge for his own death?

5. **The "ghost" from the bottom of the sea**. Many "ghost" stories have a sensible explanation. In the late 1890s the schooner *A. Ernest Mills* sank in a storm off the coast of California. A few days later the "ghost" of the schooner appeared, to the horror of the local people. The schooner had been carrying a cargo of salt when she sank. When the salt dissolved the *A. Ernest Mills* bobbed up to the surface of the ocean again. Mystery solved!

6. **The ghostly rescuer**. The first man to sail alone around the world was Joshua Slocum of Nova Scotia in Canada. He set off

in July 1895 but soon met terrible storms in the North Atlantic. After struggling to control his boat for three days Slocum gave up, exhausted. He went below to his cabin to wait for the boat to sink. He couldn't swim. Then, as the storm raged he felt the boat riding smoothly as if a strong hand was at the wheel. When he dragged himself back on deck he saw a man in fifteenth-century clothes steering the vessel. "Who are you?" he managed to ask. "I am the helmsman of the *Pinta*," the man replied. The *Pinta* was one of Christopher Columbus's ships that discovered America in 1492. Slocum found the strength to survive the storm. The fifteenth-century sailor was never seen again.

7. **The leading light**. Christopher Columbus himself had a ghostly experience at sea. When his crew were getting seriously worried about ever seeing land again, he saw a light in the sky. It was a "guiding star" that would lead them to the new world. No one else saw the light and no one believed Columbus. The next day they sighted land; they had reached the American continent.

8. **The avenging ship**. Two Arctic exploration ships, the *George Henry* and the *Rescue*, were heading for the North Pole in 1860 when they met a severe storm. The

crews decided the *Rescue* was about to sink so they abandoned her and sailed off on the *George Henry*. Two months later, as they sailed back to the point where they'd abandoned the *Rescue*, they saw a battered ship following them. It was the *Rescue*. She disappeared into the mist. But that night, as they were at anchor, the *Rescue* came back, heading straight towards the *George Henry*. She seemed to be driving ice blocks towards them – maybe as a revenge for the sailors abandoning her. Finally the derelict ship itself charged towards them. At the last second it seemed to swerve away, as if the ghostly driving force had some pity.

9. **The *Waratah* Disaster**. In July 1909 Claude Sawyer was sailing from Melbourne, Australia to London when he had terrifying dreams of a disaster. He saw himself standing at the rail of his ship, the *Waratah*, when a knight in blood-stained armour rose from the sea and mouthed the word "Waratah!" over and over again. Sawyer was so shaken that he left the ship when it reached Durban in South Africa and decided to take another ship for the second part of his journey. The *Waratah* sailed without him . . . and was never seen again. Or "probably" never seen again. Seventy years after the disappearance, an aircraft pilot reported seeing a passenger ship of the *Waratah*'s description lying on its side in clear water off the South African coast. A search was made but nothing was found. What had the pilot seen?

10. **The *Teazer* Terror**. Another ship haunting the North Atlantic was the *Young Teazer*, an American warship. In 1813 she was surrounded by warships of the British Navy. Lieutenant Johnson did not want to be captured so he blew up the *Young Teazer* . . . and himself along with it. A ship of the *Young Teazer's* description is said to sail menacingly towards ships then swerve away in flames.

THE UNEXPLAINED
The Spirit Stones

Most ghostly happenings have an explanation, natural or super-natural. But sometimes there seems to be no reason why ghostly activity should start . . . or stop.

Upper Blackwood, Australia, 1955

The sun had set but the sky was still a clear blue. The autumn nights were colder now and fuel was expensive, so the sticks that Jean Smith was gathering at the edge of the bush would cook an evening meal – and keep Gilbert and her warm through the night.

The huge farm they worked on was over 300 kilometres from the nearest city of Perth. Strangers hardly ever came this way. That was why Jean was puzzled. She felt there was a stranger nearby, watching her.

She looked around carefully. There was no one in sight. Apart from the scrub bushes there was nowhere for anyone to hide. The blank, dark windows of her wooden cabin stared out at her. They were empty.

She shivered and bent to pick up just a few more handfuls of wood before she went home. And as she bent she heard the whisper of something fly past her neck. A moment later it hit the ground with a heavy thud.

Jean didn't wait to see who was throwing stones at her. She didn't need to. She already knew there was no one there. The woman clutched her precious twigs to her chest and ran for the cottage. At her back she could feel something chasing her. There was no way she was going to turn around and look.

Wood spilled on the porch as she scrabbled at the door handle and tumbled into the cabin. Her husband looked up, wide-eyed, and saw his wife scatter the wood on the floor, slam the door and stand with her back to it. A moment later something heavy crushed into the door and almost splintered the wood.

"Spirits!" Jean hissed. "Evil spirits!"

Gilbert jumped up from his chair and wrapped a comforting arm around her shoulder. "No, Jean. We have done nothing to upset the spirits. It's more likely to be one of the shepherds having a joke."

The woman looked at him doubtfully. "There's no one out there . . . at least, no one human eyes can see."

"My eyes will see him," Gilbert assured her and he moved her gently from the door and opened it.

It was darker now. The fences were black lines against the fading grey of the pastures. The air was still. Nothing moved. In the distance a dingo howled. Somewhere closer another one answered it.

Gilbert squared his shoulders and, keeping his back to the cabin walls, walked around the outside of his home. "Hello!" he called. Only the dingo answered.

Gilbert slipped back through the door and bolted it behind him. He was just about to say something to Jean when he saw something out of the corner of his eye that made him duck. Something white rose from the corner of the room and flew towards his head. It clattered off the wall and fell to the floor. "A golf ball," he said. "One that the kids have been playing with. But how –"

Before he could finish there was a clatter on the tin roof as something heavy landed on it. "Spirits!" Jean moaned.

The man looked at his two dogs sleeping by the cold fireplace. They hadn't moved. "Those dogs know when anyone comes within a hundred yards of here," he said. "You're right, Jean – there's no one out there."

"What can we do?"

"I'll go for help," he said. "You'll be safe enough inside. Bolt the door behind me."

He snatched the keys to his old van and hurried out. As the sound of the engine faded the dogs woke up, jumped to their feet and began barking and howling. The woman slipped the chains from their necks and they threw themselves towards the door. "Get him, boy!" she said and pulled the bolt back. But when the dogs pushed through the opening door they began howling and vanished into the night.

Thud! Something hit the roof again.

Thud! That one hit the wall.

Jean Smith snatched her husband's rifle and pushed the barrel through the opening of the door. But from inside the house an empty jam jar flew across the room and splintered against the doorpost beside her head. She shut the door quickly and sat with her back to it. Every object in the room was a possible enemy now.

It was an hour before Gilbert returned with a neighbour. There had been long spells of silence when Jean had begun to relax, but as soon as she did so she was jerked back into terror by something crashing against the wall.

"Hi, Jenny!" Alf Krakour said as he came through the door. "Gilbert says you've been having a spot of bother, eh?"

Jean nodded dumbly.

"We'll soon get to the bottom of this," he promised and, taking his gun, he walked outside with her husband.

Five minutes later the men returned. Alf had stopped grinning now. "Too dark to see anything," he said. "We'll just bolt ourselves in and wait for them to get tired."

But it was Alf, Jean and Gilbert who were tired by next morning. The bombardment went on all night. When the sun rose the attack stopped.

"What do we do now?" Jean asked wearily.

"Tell the boss," Gilbert said. "Smart man, Mr Roberts. He'll sort it out."

That night Mr Roberts joined them. "Someone having a joke," he said.

"That's what I said," Gilbert put in.

"The attacks stopped in the morning because they knew you would see them throwing stuff," the ranch owner explained. He was going to say more when something hissed past his ear and clattered against the wall. The man's weather-beaten face turned pale. He bent to pick up a stone from the floor then gave a sharp cry. "It's hot!"

"Where did it come from?" Gilbert asked.

"Must have come through the wall," Roberts said.

"But there are no holes in the wall. How did it get

here?" Jean asked. The men had no answer.

"I'll find you a new cabin," the ranch-owner promised.

Gilbert Smith shook his head. "It will make no difference," he said quietly.

He walked to the window and looked out. "There's something out there," he said. "Look."

Hanging in the dark air was an unearthly light. An oval blue light. Suddenly the light moved with an eerie whistling sound and the cabin shook. Jean Smith clamped her hands over her ears but she couldn't shut the sounds out.

Slowly the sounds faded. Jean and Gilbert moved closer together. "We must learn to live with this," she said.

"Then I'll find some specialist help," their employer promised. "There's some sort of Ghost Society over in Perth. I'll contact them. See what they say." Roberts took his hat and looked carefully around the door before stepping out.

The ghost hunters from the Perth Psychic Society tried to explain to the Smiths that this sort of spirit activity was common throughout the world . . . but they couldn't stop it. "It tends to stop by itself," they said.

Jean Smith shook her head slowly. Sleepless nights and fear-filled days had shrunk her. "When? When will it stop?" she asked.

The ghost hunters shrugged. "Who knows?" they said and went away.

The woman bent wearily to gather sticks. It was autumn again. A year had passed since that first stone had been hurled at her. The sun had set but the sky was still a clear blue. The nights were colder now and fuel was expensive, so the sticks she was gathering at the edge of the bush would cook an evening meal – and keep Gilbert and her warm through the night.

She stopped and looked up. There was something wrong, something missing. For the first time in a year she smiled. She knew she *wasn't* being watched. She knew that It had gone away. Whatever *It* was had decided to leave them in peace at last.

Jean clutched the sticks and hurried back to the house. She opened the door. Gilbert looked up from his chair at the side of the fireplace. "I know," he said.

"Why?" Jean asked.

Gilbert stood up and walked across to her. He wrapped a hand around her thin shoulders. "Like the people from Perth said, 'Who knows?'"

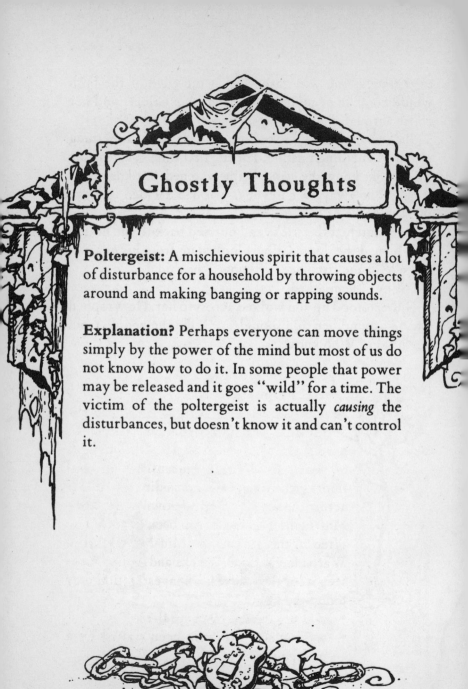

Ghostly Thoughts

Poltergeist: A mischievious spirit that causes a lot of disturbance for a household by throwing objects around and making banging or rapping sounds.

Explanation? Perhaps everyone can move things simply by the power of the mind but most of us do not know how to do it. In some people that power may be released and it goes "wild" for a time. The victim of the poltergeist is actually *causing* the disturbances, but doesn't know it and can't control it.

Many reporters visited the Smiths during their year of disturbances. They found no evidence to back the story. On the other hand, no reporter was willing to spend the night there, and most of the strange things happened at night. As many as 150 stones were said to fall on the roof on some nights.

Most of the world's ghostly experiences have been reported in Europe and particularly in the British Isles. But Australia has its own record of supernatural happenings apart from the Smith case . . .

1. **The Min-Min Light – Western Queensland**

Strange things were seen in the sky in the Smith case but such lights have been reported elsewhere in Australia for hundreds of years. In Western Queensland an oval fluorescent light is seen standing or rolling across the sky. It became known as the Min-Min Light because it has been reported so often in the area of the Min-Min Hotel in Warenda Station. Queensland police have seen it for themselves. On investigation they found the light . . .

- was not caused by camp fires
- was unlikely to have been caused by a mirage effect

• was not car headlights or their reflections. No one has ever been able to explain where the light comes from or goes to, though a farm worker reported seeing the light rising from the Min-Min graveyard around 1917. The worker was riding his horse past the graveyard and, understandably, galloped away from the place when he saw the light. To his horror the light followed him to the edge of the next town, where it mysteriously disappeared.

2. Lady's ghost – West Australia, 1953

Lady was William Courtney's greyhound. Every night the dog came to his bedroom and dropped on to the floor where it slept. One night he was half asleep when he heard the familiar sound of the dog flopping to the floor. William Courtney's hand trembled as he reached for the light switch, for that afternoon Lady had been put down by the vet following an illness. When Courtney finally found the nerve to snap on the light, the floor was empty.

3. Bluebird – Lake Eyre, 1964

Donald Campbell chose the flat salt-lake in Australia to race his car, *Bluebird*, to a new speed record. During the second run a tyre was damaged and nearly sent Campbell to his death. The support team changed the wheel but were afraid that Donald Campbell

would have lost his nerve after such a frightening experience. When they looked through the canopy he seemed perfectly calm but was staring at the screen. He went ahead with another run and broke the record. His mechanic later asked him what he'd been looking at during the wheel change. Campbell admitted he'd been looking at an image of his dead father that appeared in the screen. The image had said, "Don't worry, my boy, it will be all right." The vision had given him the courage to go on.

4. The haunted house – Newcastle, New South Wales, 1970

Michael Cooke thought he had found the perfect house for himself and his wife and baby. But they left in fear after something . . .
- made the baby sit up as if jerked by invisible hands
- rumpled bedclothes on a tidy, made-up bed
- moved toys around
- shook a door knob loudly.

But the final straw came when the ghost put in an appearance. As Michael Cooke described it, "Last night I saw a horrible white face looking out of one of the windows as I walked past. The eyes were white with green in the middle. I was so scared the tears just ran out of my eyes. That was the end. I

was thinking of buying the house but I'll never live there again."

Other tenants had reported similar problems.

THE GHOST'S REVENGE
The Miller of Chester-le-Street

Do some poor souls linger on earth? Are they tied to this world because they have some unfinished business here?

Let me tell you the story of Ann Walker. Then make up your mind.

Durham, England, 1632

The market town of Chester-le-Street stands by the River Wear. A water mill once stood down by the river. James Graham, the miller, lived by the mill in 1632.

The miller worked hard and he worked long hours. It was midnight as he put the last corn in the hopper one chill winter's night, and a damp mist rose from the river.

He came down the creaking wooden stairs and he stopped.

There was someone down there on the flour-dusted floor, yet he knew that the door of the mill had been locked.

"Who's that?" he called, peering down into the gloom. The figure made no reply. He turned up the wick of his lantern and took a step down.

He could make out the shape of a long-haired woman. And as he drew close he could see that her hair was dripping. But where the droplets hit the floor they made no mark in the thin layer of flour.

"Who are you?" he asked and the lantern trembled in his hand.

The woman raised her head. Her pale face was stained with red. It wasn't water running down her hair, but blood. The miller stared and made out four or five deep wounds that scarred her head.

No one could have such wounds and live. "Sweet Jesus,

save me!" begged the miller.

Then the woman raised her bloodied head and looked him in the eyes. "No, do not be afraid," she sighed. "I am the spirit of the murdered young Anne Walker. Sit down, sir, for you look too shocked to stand."

The miller sank down on the lowest step and placed the lantern on the old mill floor. "In God's name, tell me what you want!" he gasped.

"I want revenge," the woman said. "I cannot leave this world while my cruel murderers walk free. I need the help of you, James Graham."

"I'll do my best," the miller said.

"Then listen to my tale," the spirit said. "I lived near here in Chester-le-Street. My uncle, Joseph Walker, is a farmer. Joseph took me to his house. I worked there as his maid. But not long after, . . . I found I was with child."

The miller started to forget his fear. He shook his head in horror at her tale.

"My uncle said I'd have to go away. He said I'd have to leave to hide my shame. He promised I'd be well looked after and then return to keep his house."

"He broke his promise?" Graham asked.

"I left the house about this time of night the last new moon – two weeks ago. He sent his friend to guide me in the dark – a miner called Mark Sharp. Sharp is a tall and fearsome man. Hair black as the coal he digs and shoulders wide as a doorway. I should have been afraid of him, yet I was more afraid of travelling down that moonless road alone. We set off on the road to Durham. My guide did not have much to say. His strides were long and I stumbled as I tried to keep pace with him. I begged him to stop when we had gone five miles, and then he told me that he knew a quicker way. It meant we'd walk across the loneliest part of the moor. But I was tired, so tired, that I agreed. The road was quiet at that time of night. The moor was quieter. Only the sounds of owls and something scuttling through the rough grass. A loose sheep scared me half to death. I asked him how much farther. He told me he could see a light. He pointed to the distant hill. As I leaned forward Mark Sharp stepped behind me. He took his pick and struck me on the head. He gave these wounds that you see on my head."

Her apparition shuddered and the blood dripped to the floor. "The law will not convict those two unless we find your body," Miller Graham said.

She nodded and her hair fell forward. Quietly she told the miller where her body lay. "He threw my body in a coal pit, then he hid the pick axe in a bank nearby. He tried to wash the blood from off his shoes and stockings, but he could not get them clean, so he hid them by the pick."

The ghost began to walk towards James Graham. He scrambled to his feet and backed towards the door. "No one will believe me!" Miller Graham cried.

"But you must *try*. And try *again* until they do!" Anne Walker's ghost protested, "Or I shall haunt you till your dying day and then beyond the grave!"

The man tore at the bolts and stumbled down the moon-washed path. He dared to look behind and saw he was not followed. He hurried home and shivered in his bed.

Next day he went to work. He felt the ghost was just a dream and laughed at his own foolishness.

He did not work so late that night but left the mill before night fell. After supper he went to bed. The night was peaceful and he sank into a dreamless sleep.

When the moon came up, the spirit of the dead girl rose again. This time she was no gentle, pleading ghost. She was a threatening, fierce ghoul. She tore the sheets from the miller's bed and screamed that she wanted justice.

"Yes, Miss Walker, yes," he groaned. "Give me just one more chance. I will obey." The miller did not dare ignore her threat this time. Next morning he went to the magistrate and told his tale.

"And you say this was not a nightmare, Miller?" asked the magistrate. "And you say you had not been drinking barley wine?"

James Graham looked afraid and pitiful. He shook his head. The magistrate believed the honest man. "We'll do our best," he promised.

A search was made. At Framwellgate a disused pit was found. In the pit lay the body of Anne Walker. There were five wounds in the head. The bloody pick and shoes and stockings lay nearby, as the spirit had said.

The cruel uncle and his friend Mark Sharp were brought to trial. The men denied the charges.

At the trial Walker stood up in the dock and told some cringing lies. Yet, on the farmer's back, the judge could see a shadowy form . . . a phantom of the murdered child.

Farmer Joseph Walker and his evil friend were both found guilty and were hanged for their cruel crime.

So, those of you who say that there are no such things as ghosts, how can you explain Anne Walker's tale?

The body would have lain there still if her spirit had not guided Miller Graham to the spot. The ghost had had her revenge and she could rest in peace. So could Miller Graham.

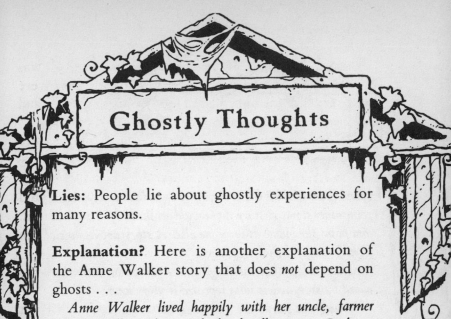

Ghostly Thoughts

Lies: People lie about ghostly experiences for many reasons.

Explanation? Here is another explanation of the Anne Walker story that does *not* depend on ghosts . . .

Anne Walker lived happily with her uncle, farmer Joseph Walker. She met the local miller, James Graham, when she took corn from the farm to his mill.

James Graham fell in love with Anne Walker. She felt nothing for him. He visited her at the farm. After a quarrel he killed her with the pickaxe that was lying in the barn.

Miller Graham took the body fives miles along the road and dropped it down a mine shaft. No one knew about his relationship with Anne Walker, so he was safe.

But he could not sleep at night. He felt guilty about the murder and was terrified of being questioned. Magistrates were looking into her disappearance.

The only way the miller could be safe would be if someone else was tried and hanged for the murder. He couldn't say, "I know where the body is because I put it there," and he couldn't leave the body undiscovered. He'd

spend the rest of his life worrying. He had to come up with some other story. A story that would get the body discovered and point the blame at someone else. A story about a visit from a vengeful ghost, perhaps?

The shadow that the judge saw could be an invention added by story-tellers who repeated it years later.

True ghost story? Or a cunning lie?

Both are possible. You must make up your own mind.

Avenging Ghosts – FACT FILE

The belief that a ghost might wander around this earth until it avenges its death is quite common. Sometimes the ghost appears to a relative, describes its death and reveals the guilty person. In some amazing cases (like the one at Chester-le-Street) no one realized the victim had died until the ghost informed them.

In many cases a ghost seems to have returned to earth for vengeance . . .

1 **The Greenbriar ghost**. Zona Shue died in West Virginia in 1897. Her husband, Edward, was in a terrible state and kept clutching at the body as the doctor was trying to examine it. In the end the doctor gave up and concluded that Zona had died of "an everlasting faint". Even when she was in her coffin Edward would let no one near her. He covered her neck with a scarf ("her favourite scarf!" he sobbed), but Zona's mother took a pillow from the coffin and tried to wash it. She found a red stain that would not come out. Then Zona's ghost appeared to her in a dream. Four nights in a row the ghost told how Edward had lost his temper and broken her neck – the ghost turned her head in a complete circle to show how loose it was! Zona's mother took the

story to the police, they examined the body and found it did indeed have a broken neck, just as the ghost had said. Edward was tried and found guilty. Zona's ghost could rest in peace, knowing justice had been done.

2. **The rapping ghost**. Louise Trafford was killed in 1949 but the police had no clues to the killer. Then a Medium called the detective in charge of the case and said she had evidence . . . from the ghost of the dead woman. The message was in the form of knocking sounds. The police didn't understand the code – it wasn't Morse code – but Louise had spent a term in prison where prisoners would send messages to each other by rapping on pipes. When one of Louise's cell-mates heard a recording of the rappings she told the police exactly what they meant. The message from beyond the grave named the killer and told the police where to find vital clues to convict him. He was arrested, tried and executed three months later.

3. **The Iverawe ghost**. Duncan Campbell was the Lord of Inverawe in Scotland. One night in 1748 he gave a stranger shelter. He didn't know that the stranger had just murdered his cousin, Donald. But Donald's ghost appeared and told the Lord of Inverawe that the murderer was in the house: "Blood has been shed. Do not shield

the murderer." The Lord of Inverawe ignored the ghost's message four times that night. Finally the ghost said, "Farewell – until we meet again at Ticonderoga." Ten years passed. No one had ever heard of Ticonderoga. Lord Duncan joined the British Army and was sent to fight the French in north-east America. At Fort Carillon he learned that the native Americans called the place Ticonderoga. He knew he was going to die and told his friends. In a vicious battle many men died and Lord Duncan received a slight wound from a musket. He felt he had escaped, but ten days later the wound had turned septic. He died and the ghost's revenge was complete.

4. **The Fox family ghost**. A family called Fox lived near New York. There was farmer James Fox, his wife and two daughters, Maggie and Katie. In 1848 their house was disturbed by strange banging noises in the night. The girls discovered they could communicate with a disturbed spirit through

rapping – one rap for "yes", two for "no".
Eventually they learned that the rappings
came from the spirit of a man called Charles
Rosma. Rosma told how he was murdered
and buried in the cellar. When neighbours
helped the Fox family to dig in the cellar
they found human hair and bones. The spirit
said he was murdered by a Mr Bell, but that
the killer would never be brought to justice.
Mr Bell, who had lived in the house five
years before the Fox family, was very angry
and denied it. The case caused such a
sensation in the press that the Fox girls
became famous and appeared all over
America. The Spiritualist movement started
in America and many people copied the
performances of the Fox girls. After forty
years of fame Katie admitted it was all a
trick, but the Spiritualists refused to believe
her!

GHOSTLY DREAMS
George's Dream

George and Hart were brothers who lived in Cornwall, England. They were not just brothers but very close friends too.

George became a sailor and they were separated for the first time in their lives. In February 1840 George's ship reached the island of St Helena. While he was there he had a horrific dream. This is his story . . .

Cornwall, England, 1840

I dreamed that my brother, Hart, was at Trebodwina market and that I was with him. I was quite close by his side during the whole of his buying and selling. I could see and hear everything that went on around me. But I felt it wasn't my body that was travelling round with him; it was my shadow or my spirit. Hart didn't seem to know that I was there.

Hart spoke to people and they replied. I could hear it all. But when I tried to speak no one heard me and no one replied.

I felt that this was a sign of some hidden danger that was going to befall him but I knew I wouldn't be able to stop the danger because I had no way of warning him. All I could do was stand by helplessly and watch.

My brother Hart had a very successful day at the market and made a large sum of money. I should have felt happy for him but all I felt was fear. As the sun set he began to make his way homeward on his horse. My shadow followed him and my terror grew as he reached the village of Polkerrow.

Polkerrow is no longer a village. It is just a collection of deserted cottages round the cross-roads. No one lives there now. It was quiet and the setting sun was casting long shadows over the road. I was frantic. I wanted to warn Hart in some way that he must go no further.

Then I noticed two long shadows moving across the path. Two men appeared from one of the deserted cottages. It seemed they had been waiting there. I knew them well – they were the Hightwood brothers. They were villainous poachers who lived in a lonely wood near St Eglos. I also knew that it was Hart they were waiting for.

The men said, "Good evening, master," very politely.

"Good evening," Hart replied. "I had been meaning to call on you," he said. It seemed he didn't sense the danger. My shadow was screaming out, "Ride on! Ride on now before it is too late." But Hart did not hear any warning.

"I have some animals I want taking to market next week," Hart said.

"So why not pay us now, Mr Northey?" the older Hightwood said.

That was the first time Hart began to sense they meant no good.

"I cannot pay for work that has not yet been done," he said.

"Ah, but you can, Mr Northey," the younger Hightwood said. He was standing by my brother's saddle. The older man walked to the horse's head and took hold of the horse's reins. "We need the money now," he said.

"Come to my house and I'll see if I can loan you some," Hart said. The horse could feel my brother's nervousness and started prancing in the dust.

The older man was holding the horse's head firmly. He said, "Mr Northey, we know you have just come from Trebodwina market. And we also know you have plenty of money in your pockets. We are desperate men and you aren't leaving this place until we've got that money. So hand it over."

Hart did not reply. He lashed at the man with his whip and spurred the horse on. The man fell back but held on to the reins.

The younger poacher immediately drew a pistol and fired. He was standing close to my brother's side. He could not miss. I watched as Hart dropped lifeless from the saddle. The poachers tied the horse to a tree in the orchard. Then they stole the money from Hart's pockets and dragged his body up the stream. They hid him under the overhanging bushes.

The poachers returned to the road and covered up the marks on the road. They hid the pistol in the thatched roof of a disused cottage by the roadside and returned home to

their own house in the woods.

My ship left St Helena and sailed for Plymouth. All the way home I was sure that my brother had been murdered in the way I'd seen in my dream. When I reached home two months later my father was waiting at the quayside. "I know what you have come to tell me," I said. "It's Hart, isn't it?"

"Yes," my father said.

"He was robbed and murdered two months ago."

My father nodded. "You were always close to Hart," he said. "It is no surprise that you sensed his death."

And he told me the details of the crime. They were exactly as I had seen in my dream.

"The whole county was shocked by the brutal murder," my father said. "The authorities were determined to bring the murderers to justice. Two poachers called Hightwood have been arrested. Their cottage has been searched and blood-stained clothes found. 'From skinning rabbits,' the brothers claimed. But there was no pistol. The younger

Hightwood said he had owned a gun years ago, but had lost it," he went on.

"The Hightwoods were taken to the magistrates' court. There wasn't much evidence against them. That murder weapon is still missing. But the men acted in a guilty manner. They were sent for trial anyway," my father explained.

"In that case I think I can help avenge my brother's murder. For I can tell you where the gun is hidden. The gun is in the thatch of the cottage by the roadside." I said.

That was George's story. He could have been lying about dreaming the murder – after all, the men had already been arrested and their story was known to everyone.

But when the roof was searched the gun was found, exactly as in the dream.

"How did you know?" George was asked.

"Because I saw it in a dream," he answered.

"And when did you have this dream?"

"I had the dream on the very night my brother was murdered, though I was two thousand miles away."

Faced with the weapon, the Hightwoods confessed to the murder. They hoped that the confession would save their lives and they'd be sent to prison. It didn't work.

A month later they were hanged for their crime.

Ghostly Thoughts

Doubles: The image of a living person is seen by a friend or relative when they are many miles away. This is usually at a time of trouble for the "double", maybe when they are on the point of death.

Explanation? Perhaps everyone is a mind-reader. As well as seeing, touching, smelling or hearing other people maybe we can also sense their thoughts when those thoughts are very emotional. Our sight and hearing only allow us to sense people so far and no further, but thoughts can travel hundreds or even thousands of miles.

In the story of the Northey brothers the "ghost" was the living relative. His spirit seems to have left his body and travelled thousands of miles to be at the scene of the crime.

Another type of ghostly vision is when the ghost of the dead person visits a relative (or friend or loved one) at the time of their death. These ghost stories are called "point of death" visions. Many thousands have been recorded over the years . . .

1. **The Last Goodbye**. Rod Nielson lived in San Diego in California. He was very close to his father, Henry. Old Henry loved his grand-daughter Katie but seemed sad when he heard that Rod's wife was having another grandchild. He hinted that he wouldn't be around to see his new grandson. He was quite, quite sure that the unborn baby would be a boy. In the summer of 1972 Rod was in his office when he clearly heard his father say, "Well, I guess that's it, son. Give Katie a kiss from me. Goodbye." Rod turned and saw an image of his father in a checked shirt and old trousers. In Henry's hand was a garden trowel and a bunch of marigolds. No one else in the office saw a thing. Rod hurried to his father's house. Henry was lying dead on the lawn wearing the same

clothes as in the vision. In one hand he held a garden trowel, in the other a bunch of marigolds. But that's not the end of the story. For when the baby was born it *was* a boy. Rod turned to young Katie and said, "Pity Granddad couldn't be here to see it." Katie shook her head, "But Daddy," she said, "Granddad *is* here, standing next to Mummy. Can't you see him?"

2. **The Tugboat disaster**. Not all ghosts appear at the "moment of death". Mrs Paquet of Chicago walked into her pantry and saw a clear image of her brother. He appeared to trip over a rope and vanish over a low railing. She knew that he was working on a tugboat in Chicago Harbour at the time. Mrs Paquet dropped her cup of tea and cried, "My God! Ed is drowned!" She eventually received news that this had in fact happened, but it had happened six hours before her vision.

3. **The Woman in White**. One of the most chilling ghosts must be the one that foretells your own death. In 1837 John Allen saw something which told him he was about to die. He was miserable for the next six months but he would never say why. Then, one day while he was at work, his daughter Polly saw a woman dressed in white walking down the hill towards her. No one else saw the woman and Polly's sister laughed at her. "People don't wear white dresses on a working day," she said. Later that day they learned that their father had drowned while he was working on the river. He died at the time Polly had seen the woman. She had not seen the dying person at the moment of his death, as in most stories, but had she seen the ghost her father had met just months before?

4. **The Ghostly Car**. At 11.30 p.m. on 4 May 1980, Joseph Hannah's father heard Joseph's car pull into the driveway at their home. He knew the sound of that car engine and the sounds his son made parking his car. He fell asleep, content that his son was home safely. At 11.30 p.m. on 4 May 1980 Joseph Hannah's girlfriend saw him driving down the main street of her town. He waved and smiled at her, then drove on. She was a little surprised because she had watched him set off home at 11 p.m. At 11.30 p.m. on 4 May

1980 Joseph Hannah's baby-sitter heard footsteps pacing in the baby's room. Three people thought they'd seen or heard Joseph at 11.30 that night, but none of them had. He had died at 11.10 that evening when his car was wrecked by a landslide.

5. **The White Room**. Some vision stories have a happy ending. In the 1850s a little girl was walking along a country lane not far from her home. Slowly the lane faded from sight and all she could see was a bedroom in her house known as the White Room. Her mother was lying, still, on the floor. Instead

of going home the girl went straight to the doctor and persuaded him to go home with her. They found her mother, in the White Room, suffering from a heart attack. The doctor saved her life. It seems as if the mother's spirit had carried a "panic" message to her daughter.

GHOSTLY RETURNS
The Lives and Deaths of Jane

Have you ever visited a place and felt that you've been there before, even though you know you haven't? Many people have that feeling. One explanation is that you really have been there before . . . in another life. Perhaps we have all lived many lives before, but we've forgotten them. However, if we are hypnotized we might just remember our past lives . . .

Cardiff, Wales, 1974

"I shall count slowly backwards from ten. When I reach zero you will be asleep. Do you understand?"

The woman nodded. Her feet were up on the couch but she wasn't relaxed. Her bright eyes were fixed on the old man. "Yes, doctor," she said. Her voice was thin with a musical Welsh accent.

He looked at her. "No, Jane, not yet. You're still a little too excited. You've been hypnotized many times before. You know you have to relax."

She closed her eyes and took a deep breath. After a minute she said, "I'm ready."

The man's voice was smooth and soothing as he began to count slowly. "Ten . . . your eyelids are heavy . . . nine . . . you can feel them closing . . . eight . . . you are going to sleep . . . seven . . . all you can hear is my voice . . . six . . . your body is so heavy it is sinking through the couch . . . five . . . your breathing is slower . . . four . . . you will be asleep when I say 'zero' . . . three . . . but you will still hear my voice . . . two . . . you are slipping . . . one . . . zero."

Jane's eyes were closed, her mouth slightly open and her body limp. The man spoke briskly. "Now, Jane, we have done this before. I'm going to ask you to go back in time. Back to the days before you were born. Back to when you lived another life in another body. Do you remember?"

"Yes-s," she replied with a tired slur to her voice.

"But this time will be different, won't it?"

"Yes."

"In the past I have told you which date I wanted you to return to. We went back to Roman Britain, didn't we?"

"Yes . . . I was called Livonia," the woman said dreamily.

"And in Tudor England you were the maid of honour to a princess," the man went on. His eyes behind the spectacles were sharp as a bird's.

"This time I want *you* to choose. Of all the lives you've lived before, is there one that stands out in your memory?"

The woman's limp face tensed in a frown. Her soft breathing became harsh and her limp hands were clenched into fists. The white-haired man leaned forward. "Let it happen, Jane . . . relax."

As he watched the woman changed. Her face became alive and her eyes flew open. The slack chin grew tight and she lifted it proudly.

The man asked, "Who are you?"

"Rebecca," the woman replied quickly. Her voice was firm and there was no trace of the Welsh accent Jane had.

"Where do you live, Rebecca?"

"York," she said.

"The year?"

"In Christian years it is 1189."

"Tell me about your life," he urged softly.

The Rebecca character spoke quickly as if she were irritated by the questions, or too busy to stop and answer them. "It's such a hard life for us."

"You're poor?"

Her lips pursed in anger. "Of course not. My husband is a wealthy merchant. It's hard because we're Jewish."

"I see," the old man nodded and sat back a little.

"They hate us," she said and an angry spot of red coloured each cheek. "The Christians can't lend money . . . it's against the law . . . but we Jews can. They come to us to borrow and they hate us because they owe us. They make us wear yellow badges on our clothes. They hate us. The Christians blame us for everything. Two hundred of them died in a plague last summer, but no Jews died. They say that is our fault too. They want to kill us!"

"Why do you say that?"

"There were riots in London and Lincoln and Chester. They killed Jews then. York will be next. I fear for my children. My little Rachel is only eleven. What will happen to her?"

The woman twisted her hands in worry and her face was creased with suffering.

The man leaned forward and spoke slowly. "Rebecca, time has moved on. When we last spoke you were worried about being attacked. What has happened?"

Now the woman's face was pale. Her eyes were staring. "Hush! Keep your voice down. They will hear us."

"Sorry," the man said quietly. "Where are you?"

"We are in the Christian church near Coppergate, hiding in a cellar. If they find us they will murder us."

"What happened?"

"We woke to the smell of burning . . . they'd come in the night and set fire to Benjamin's house next door. They killed his wife and children and carried off all his treasure. So we put all our money in bags and fled to the castle for safety."

"Did you reach it?"

"They followed us. Through the dark streets they chased us. They were carrying torches and screaming they wanted us burned. My husband, Joseph, took a knife and split a sack of money. The silver spilled out on the road. The mob stopped to pick it up. We reached the castle and we stood inside with all the other Jews of York."

"The mob couldn't get you in the castle," the hypnotist said.

"Oh, but they could. They began battering at the door. Some parents began to kill their own children rather than let the mob get their hands on them."

"But you didn't kill Rachel?"

"No. Oh, no. We used the last of our money to bribe a guard. He let us out of a secret door before the mob broke down the gates. Now we're hiding in this church. They tell us King John has ordered the murder of all Jews in England! It's not just the people who are chasing us now, it's the soldiers too. Joseph has gone for food. He's been such a long time. Now Rachel is crying – hush, Rachel, they'll hear us! Listen! Horses. I can hear horses."

"Perhaps it's Joseph returning with food," the white-haired man said.

"Joseph didn't have a horse. No . . . I can hear their footsteps now. They're coming for us. They're shouting, 'Kill the Jews, kill the Jews!' They're searching the church now. God protect us! Hush, Rachel, don't cry. Only the priest knows we're down here. A priest will not betray us . . . but listen . . . I can hear the sound of the stone floor being lifted. He's told them where we are . . . they're coming . . . no, not Rachel! Not my Rachel! Don't take my child . . . no-o-o!" the woman wailed, a long and terrified cry.

The hypnotist was shocked. "They haven't taken her, have they? They're not going to harm you, are they?"

But the woman's tortured face was blank now. Her eyes stared, sightless. She whispered just one word. So soft that the man hardly heard it. "Dark," she sighed.

The man was trembling a little as he said, "Jane? Jane?"

The woman on the couch was limp again. Her eyes closed.

"Jane, I'm going to count to three. On the count of three you will wake up. You will be Jane Evans and the year is 1974. One . . . two . . . three!"

The woman opened her eyes slowly. She smiled at the

man and her voice was bright with that Welsh accent. "What happened, doctor?" she said. "Why, doctor, are you all right? Was it something I said? You look like *death*!"

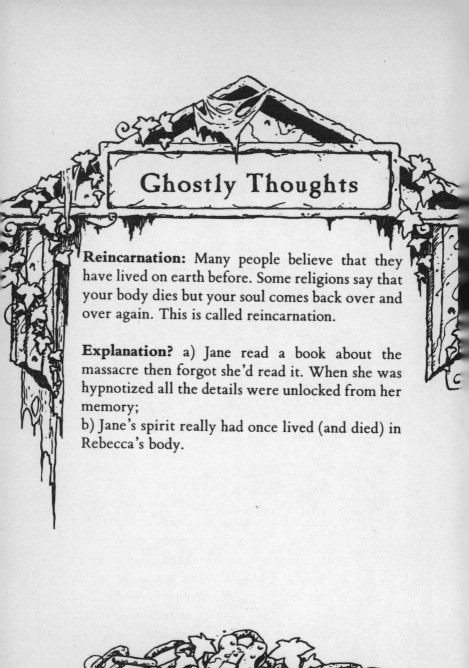

Ghostly Thoughts

Reincarnation: Many people believe that they have lived on earth before. Some religions say that your body dies but your soul comes back over and over again. This is called reincarnation.

Explanation? a) Jane read a book about the massacre then forgot she'd read it. When she was hypnotized all the details were unlocked from her memory;
b) Jane's spirit really had once lived (and died) in Rebecca's body.

Ghostly Returns – FACT FILE

Some people have seen their past lives in dreams or under hypnosis. But are they real? There are arguments for and against.

The case for reincarnation
1. Jane Evans' story was checked by a historian. Many of the facts were correct, and they were the sort of things an ordinary housewife like Jane would not know. Where did she get the facts from if she didn't get them from the memory of a past life?
2. "Rebecca" described hiding in the cellar of a church near Coppergate in York. But historians said the church nearest Coppergate had no cellar. Then, six months after Jane Evans' tape was made, workmen found a cellar just where she'd said it was. How could she have known about the cellar when no one else in this century knew?
3. Some people claim that they learn things in one life and keep that skill in their next life. A man who was a great piano player died. His spirit then entered the body of a baby who grew up to be a brilliant piano player at the age of three years old! That baby was the famous musician, Mozart. How else did he learn so quickly?

The case against reincarnation

1. An investigator looked closely into Jane Evans's story and decided that much of her information was incorrect about York and Jews of that time. The researcher also discovered that a lot of her information came from a play that had been broadcast on BBC Radio.

2. Another of Jane Evans' "characters" was Livonia, who lived in Roman Britain. Much of her story came word for word from a novel called *The Living Wood* by Louis de Wohl. It seems Jane forgot that she'd read the book but the details were there in the back of her mind. This is something called "secret memory" that everybody seems to have.

3. A lot of the remembered "characters" are famous people with interesting stories to tell. Surely the chances of being a king or a queen must be millions to one. A 1980s tour guide in Egypt once complained that, in the dozens of American tourists on that trip, he had *nine* Cleopatras!

GHOSTLY MESSENGERS
Diary of a Haunting

Some ghosts seem doomed to wander the earth because they need to tell someone something before they leave. It can take years – hundreds of years – before they find the right person to listen. Not everyone can "tune in" to a ghost. It seems that some people, especially nervous people, can attract a ghost to tell its story. In the case of the haunting at Ash Manor in Sussex the ghost had a long wait before it found the right person . . .

The Diary of Elizabeth Keller, aged 16 years and three months

23 June 1934

Our last night in the old house. I do hope we'll be happy in the new one. It's called Ash Manor and it is beautiful. Father took us to see it yesterday. So peaceful. I'm sure father and mother will be happier once we settle in.

It's been hard for them, I know. Father's been so miserable. I'm not sure quite why. The doctor says it's something called "depression". I think it's the strain of running his business. Everyone is having trouble making money these days. I think that's why the last owners of Ash Manor sold it; they needed the money. Anyway, Father says it was very cheap.

Once we move in he'll have that lovely old house to come home to at night.

I can't wait.

24 June 1934

The end of our first day. The servants have been working very hard to make the house ready for us. It's so large I have my own bedroom and writing room. That's where I'm writing this diary.

The vicar, Mr Twist, said the oldest part of Ash Manor dates back to the thirteenth century and the reign of Edward the Confessor. I know from my history lessons that Edward the Confessor was king in the eleventh century. But it would have been rude to correct the good man so I held my tongue.

Most of the house is only about a hundred years old, though. Mr Twist says the original building began to crumble and was rebuilt by a Victorian owner. But I live in the oldest part.

It's so thrilling to know I'm surrounded by six hundred (or eight hundred) years of history! Hope I'm not too excited to sleep.

25 June 1934

I'm tired. I didn't sleep too well. I know the servants still had lots of unpacking and sorting to do, but I didn't expect them to be up half of the night doing it.

I spoke to the maid quite sharply at breakfast.

"Metcalfe."

"Yes, Miss Keller?" she said.

"What time did you get to bed last night?"

"I beg your pardon?" she said, surprised.

"I heard you moving about in the servants' quarters till all hours," I complained.

She couldn't look me in the face. Her hand was shaking as she served my scrambled egg. "Sorry, Miss, but we was all asleep by midnight," she muttered.

Metcalfe was lying, of course. I could tell that father had been disturbed by them too. His face was grey with fatigue and there were purplish shadows under his eyes.

He seemed very much withdrawn. Hardly spoke. I'm

sure he'll be better when he's settled in and had a good night's sleep.

Mother and I explored the gardens of Ash Manor today. They'll be beautiful when the gardeners have finished. A fine place to sit and read. We had tea on the lawn, though it needs cutting.

Father was late home from work and we have all gone to bed early. I hope I sleep better tonight.

26 June 1934

Another night with very little sleep, and everyone's nerves are getting frayed. I got out of bed at midnight to climb to the servants' quarters and complain about their tramping about in the middle of the night. But the servants were nowhere to be seen. The sounds were those of footsteps on floorboards and they seemed to be coming from the attic.

This morning I asked Almond, the butler, about the footsteps.

"No, Miss Keller, there are no floorboards in the attic," he said. "The servants heard nothing," he added quickly. But I know he's lying. They're trying to hide something. When father came down he looked worse than ever. I asked him about it.

"Nothing to bother yourself about, Elizabeth," he said.

But when I persisted, he said, "The servants seem to think the place is haunted. They've been talking to the shopkeepers in the village about some old legends. All nonsense, of course. The last people to live here had no problems – and they lived here for seven years. And the ones before for thirteen. It's all nonsense. Probably just jackdaws roosting in the attic. We'll get someone to sort them out. Now get on with your breakfast." But I wasn't hungry.

I asked Mr Twist, the vicar, about the stories and he laughed. But it wasn't a very happy laugh. He made some excuse and left very quickly.

27 June 1934
I'm so tired. I don't think I slept more than two hours. I'd fallen asleep at ten o'clock but was wakened at midnight by the most terrible fuss in the corridor outside the bedroom. Father was standing at the door to Mother's room and babbling something. I ran across and said, "What's wrong?"

"Help me get him into the library," Mother said, and we led him downstairs. Mother poured him a large glass of brandy and made him drink it while I rubbed his cold and shaking hand.

"Go back to bed, Elizabeth," Mother ordered.

"No, let her stay," Father put in. "She needs to hear this too. She's sixteen now, you know."

"I know how old my daughter is, thank you," Mother snapped. "I simply think we should not burden her with the problems of your nerves."

Father looked up angrily and I was afraid they were going to start one of their terrible rows. His breathing was short and tense but he kept his voice low. "It was not my nerves, Alice," he said. "You admit you heard it too!"

Mother gave a sharp nod. Father turned to me. "I was lying awake, reading, when I heard the most fearful bangs on my door. Three bangs. But when I opened it there was no one there. I went to your mother's room. She heard them too. I didn't imagine it. There is nothing wrong with my nerves. Nothing. Nothing!"

"Of course not, Father," I soothed him.

But none of us could get back to sleep.

28 June 1934

And now my father has seen it. This time I heard the knock on his door. I hurried from my room and saw my father standing there, clinging to the doorpost in fear. When we got him into the library this time he said, "I've seen him . . . it . . . I've seen the thing that's been making the noise."

"Hush!" Mother said. "You'll frighten Elizabeth."

"I need to know," I said. "Go on, Father. What was it?"

He swallowed thirstily at the brandy and let out a low sigh. "Standing in the doorway was a man. An oldish man – older than me, dressed in one of those things peasants used to wear on farms."

"A smock," my mother said.

"Aye, a smock. A green smock. And his trousers were muddy, as if he'd just come from the fields. He had a shapeless hat on his head and a sort of scarf around his throat. I thought it was one of the gardeners. I asked him what he wanted. He didn't seem to hear me. Didn't answer. So I went to grab his shoulder, but my hand went clean through it. I fell back against the doorpost almost in a faint. When I opened my eyes again he'd gone."

"We'll see what Mr Twist has to say about this," Mother said. "The vicar will soon rid us of this . . . thing."

I was surprised. Mother has always blamed my father's "nerves" for everything. "You think there is something, Mother?" I asked carefully.

She looked at me and her eyes were dark-shadowed like

father's. "I . . . I heard the knock too."

"You went to your door?"

"I went to my door," she said.

"And you saw the ghost?"

Perhaps I shouldn't have used that word. Mother's lips went pale and tight. "I saw . . . something," she admitted. "I saw it walk towards the fireplace in your father's room. I'm sure there's something hidden in that chimney."

"What else, Mother?" I asked.

"It raised its head . . . I saw what lay beneath that scarf around its neck."

"What was it, Mother?"

She looked at me. "Pray you never see it, child!"

2 July 1934

So much has happened I haven't had the time to keep this diary up to date. Mr Twist came with his prayers and sprinkling of holy water. "Exorcism," he called it. That seemed to annoy the ghost. It's becoming bolder. I have seen it for myself.

So have the servants and that is why Metcalfe is leaving. We are becoming desperate, so desperate that we have called in a spiritualist – someone who can talk to spirits, see who it is, find out what it wants.

I sleep in Mother's bedroom now and we pray. That seems to help. I hope this spiritualist can end our misery.

4 July 1934

Mr Twist said it is mumbo-jumbo. He doesn't believe in spiritualism. But it was so amazing. The medium was Mrs Garrett, a small Irish woman about Mother's age.

She walked in the front door and stopped. "Ah, yes," she said. "I can feel the problem."

"Poppycock!" Mr Twist muttered, but she ignored him.

"There is pain. There is suffering here," she said. She had a slight Irish accent.

Mrs Garrett wandered round the house then came to the oldest part. "Here," she said. "We will try to talk to him here."

"What should we do?" Father asked nervously.

"Sit around the table," she ordered. "Draw the curtains."

"That'll be so we can't see any tricks or jiggery-pokery," Mr Twist whispered to me.

When we were sitting in the gloom lit by just one candle, Mrs Garrett said she had a link with the world of spirits, in particular a spirit called Uvani. We should not be bothered if she seemed to change during the session.

She closed her eyes. All I could hear was Mr Twist's breathing. Even he was fascinated. At last Mrs Garret opened her eyes. When she spoke her voice was stronger and she had no Irish accent. It seems it was the spirit of Uvani speaking to us.

"There is a man who wishes to speak to you. The man who is haunting this house."

"Who is he?" mother said quickly.

"His name is Charles Edward . . . and he has suffered much from imprisonment," Mrs Garrett (or Uvani) replied.

"Was he imprisoned here?" Mr Twist put in. "This house was never a prison."

Uvani seemed to be talking to Charles Edward a few moments then spoke to us. "No. The prison was near here but not in this house."

"Then why does he come here?" the vicar asked.

"Charles Edward is suffering and he felt some living soul suffering in this house. Suffering attracts suffering like a magnet."

We knew Uvani meant Father and his nervous problem. We said nothing.

"Who imprisoned him?" Mr Twist asked.

"The king – King Edward, his half-brother," Uvani replied.

"Which King Edward? The fourth or the fifth?"

Uvani nodded and simply said, "Yes."

"Hah! That's a nonsense reply," the vicar snapped. That seemed to destroy the spell. The spiritualist blinked and the spirit of Uvani left her.

Mrs Garrett will return tomorrow and then we speak to Charles Edward himself.

5 July 1934

Mrs Garrett's face changed when Charles Edward took over her body. We all gasped. For her face became the face of the man in green, and her voice was a man's voice. "A trick," Mr Twist said. I wasn't so sure. Charles Edward spoke.

"I am half-brother to the king, but my followers believe I have more right to the throne than Edward. They started a rebellion and put me at the head. I didn't really want the crown, I just wanted my land back. I was robbed of my land by the Earl of Huntingdon. Of course Edward won. He locked me up here and left me to rot in gaol."

"Which king?" Mr Twist said softly.

"Edward."

"Which Edward?"

"Edward," was all the spirit would say.

"Why do you haunt this house?" the vicar asked.

"I need help – help me to take my revenge. Revenge on the friends who betrayed me; revenge on the brother who tortured me."

"They are all dead," Mr Twist said. "Long, long dead."

"I want my revenge!" the spirit cried and it brought tears to my eyes to hear him. To me he was as real a person as Mother or Father. "I will not leave until I have had my revenge."

Father gave a great sigh and buried his face in his hands. "We'll never be free of this haunting."

6 July 1934

I do not like Mr Twist, but he spoke a lot of sense today.

"The woman is a fraud," he said. "She makes money by putting on performances like she did last night."

"We paid her well," Mother admitted.

"I know a lot of local history," the vicar went on. "Mrs Garret's story was a powerful one, but a nonsense. Did you notice how she refused to name the king? I have checked all the record books and this rebellion simply never happened."

"So what is this ghost? We didn't imagine him. We've all seen him. Another servant left today," Mother said.

"I think Mrs Garrett said one thing that made sense. She said that suffering attracts suffering. Mr Keller is clearly unhappy. It is his unhappiness which is creating the haunting. This house is haunted because Mr Keller wants it to be haunted."

I looked at Father. He didn't deny it. "But who is the green man?"

"The green man is not the long-lost brother of a long-dead king. The green man only lived in one place. He was created in the mind of your unhappy father. Once your father finds happiness the green man will disappear." The vicar turned to Father. "See a doctor, Mr Keller, then come to church and find peace." He turned to Mother and me. "And you have your parts to play. Suffering attracts suffering – but remember, happiness attracts happiness. Be happy."

We talked long into the night. We resolved to try. We will help one another. Together we can destroy this ghostly green man.

7 July 1934
Last night I slept peacefully for the first time since we moved here. The green man is gone, driven away by the one weapon he couldn't face. Happiness.

Ghostly Thoughts

Spirits: The "souls" of dead people who don't want to leave this world. The spirit wants to talk to a friend or relative by a) appearing as a vision (often in a dream) and giving a message; b) finding a sensitive person to carry their message – a "medium". They speak through the mouth of that medium. Sometimes these spirits are friendly and want to pass on advice or warnings to their loved ones.

Explanation? The living may simply dream the vision. Many "mediums" have been caught out in their cheating over the years. Remember, they are often well paid!

Fakes – FACT FILE

The Ash Manor case is interesting. The ghostly appearance of the green man seems to be a truly ghostly happening, but the attempt to talk to the ghost through a "medium" seems to have been a trick.

In the history of ghosts there have been a lot of tricksters making a lot of money from frauds and fakes. Some unhappy people want to talk to a loved one who is dead. A "medium" will claim to put them in touch with the dead person and pass on messages, but could simply pretend to pass on their messages and invent the replies they want to hear.

In Ancient Greece you could talk to the gods through the "medium" of a priest and receive replies. Even today mediums can fill large theatres with hundreds of people who believe they are in touch with the afterlife.

Sadly there is a long history of fakes.

1. **The ghostbuster**. Harry Houdini was a very skilled magician whose special trick was escaping – from handcuffs, boxes, coffins, safes and even prisons. Houdini desperately wanted to get in touch with his dead mother. He spent years looking for a genuine medium but all he found were fakes. Being a great magician himself he could work out all the tricks they used.

2. **The ghostly cabinet**. The American Davenport Brothers used a special cabinet in their performances in the 1860s. They were tied up and locked in the cabinet. On the darkened stage ghostly hands reached from the cabinet and played musical instruments. When the cabinet was opened they were found to be tied up as tightly as ever. Many people saw this as proof of a spirit world and no one ever caught them trying to cheat. A religion called Spiritualism grew up in the nineteenth century from such contacts with the dead. Many other mediums began to copy the cabinet idea. Before Ira Davenport died he confessed to Harry Houdini that it was all a clever fraud, and showed him the conjuring tricks the brothers had used.

3. **The fairy photographs**. Sir Arthur Conan Doyle was the writer of the Sherlock Holmes detective stories and a great believer in spiritualism. He was shown photographs of fairies taken by two girls in Yorkshire. He was quite sure that the photographs proved that fairies existed and never considered that two girls aged ten and sixteen could create cunning trick photographs. Doyle and thousands of others believed the pictures were real. They weren't! The "fairies" in the pictures were paper cutouts. The sisters finally admitted their trick sixty years later, long after Doyle's death.

4. **The solid ghost**. Mediums can produce rapping noises and make tables rise from the floor. But their most amazing skill is to make a ghost "materialize" – take a solid form and walk round the room. The medium will usually step inside a cabinet and close the curtains. In the darkened room a spot of white will appear in front of the curtains and grow into a cloud. A face will emerge from the cloud and finally the whole ghost. The ghost can walk around the room and touch the visitors, who may find the spirit solid and warm. An author called Robert Chaney explained that the solid ghost is formed from "ectoplasm" – part of the medium's own body flows out of her mouth and forms a second body that the ghost steps into. The truth is that the solid "ghost" is just the medium in a different dress. The top dress is taken off behind the curtains; the medium is wearing a second one painted in luminous paint underneath. The "cloud" is a piece of fine white material that the medium has hidden, usually in her knickers!

Perhaps the most famous case of fraud is the Cock Lane ghost of the 1760s in London . . .

POLTERGEISTS
The Cock Lane Ghost

Most ghosts are harmless. Miserable to themselves, frightening to other people, but harmless.

The only sorts of ghosts that seem dangerous are "poltergeists". A poltergeist is a spirit that often begins by making rapping noises but gradually gets more violent. Objects are thrown around a room and people may be lifted into the air.

Many poltergeists have one thing in common. They appear in a room where a teenager is living. Some scientists say the poltergeist is in fact the spirit of that teenager. Because the young person is growing up they lose control of the spirit inside them. This "out of control spirit" is so strong it can move objects. The trouble is that because it is "out of control" the teenager can't "switch on" the poltergeist whenever s/he wants. That means it can't be tested very easily.

If you were a teenager with poltergeist problems you'd get a lot of attention. If you enjoyed that attention then you might want the disturbances to go on. How do you do that? Sometimes you have to cheat. The trouble is, if you are caught cheating just once then no one will ever believe there was a true poltergeist spirit.

That's what happened to little Lizzie Parsons . . .

London, England, 1762

The room was dim. It was hot. There were too many people crowded in it to meet the famous Cock Lane Ghost.

They shuffled and sniffed, they coughed and they muttered the odd word here and there. Some sat on chairs around the bed. Some stood. No one leaned against the wooden walls. They'd heard the stories. There was something there, behind the walls. Something strange and menacing.

There was a bed against one wall, and in the bed lay a

girl of about thirteen – a small girl with wide eyes over a snub nose and pale cheeks. Lizzie Parsons.

A thin man in a black coat spoke quietly. "The ghost will be here soon, ladies and gentlemen," he said. He said it for the fifth time. Someone sighed.

"It's not there, Pa," the girl said. "Too many people in the room, I think."

Some people groaned and grumbled.

"Sorry, I'll have to ask you to leave," Richard Parsons said.

There was a clattering of chairs and louder grumbles as the watchers rose and wandered out of the door. Finally there were just three men in the room with Richard Parsons and his daughter, Lizzie.

The large man with a red face turned to Richard Parsons. "So they are all lies, are they? All these stories you've been spreading about me are lies, eh?"

Parsons wrung his hands. "I've said nothing about you, Will Kent. "It's the spirit. The spirit has been saying those things. You can't blame me!"

"But I do blame you, Parsons," the big man said, and his face turned a darker red. "I even read about myself in the newspaper. Read about the things you said I'd done."

Will Kent took a step forward and Parsons backed away. The big man's hand clenched into a fist. He began to raise it. Parsons whimpered and turned his head away. Suddenly there was a sharp noise.

Rap!

Will Kent looked round quickly. The two men who were with him shrugged their shoulders. "The spirit!" Parsons squeaked. "The spirit is ready to speak! Sit down, Kent; sit down Minister; sit down, Doctor." Parsons fussed them like a hen with chicks until they were seated in a half-circle round the bed.

Little Lizzie lay perfectly still in the bed, her eyes fixed on the ceiling. Her father spoke quietly but clearly. "Are you there, spirit?"

Rap!

"That means, 'yes'," Parsons explained quickly. "It's two raps for 'no'."

The visitors looked around the room. The noise seemed to have come from the wall behind them. The minister crossed himself quickly. The doctor looked puzzled. Kent looked at Parsons with hatred.

"Oh, spirit, have you a message for us?" Parsons asked.

Rap!

"Will you tell us who you are, spirit?"

Rap!

"Are you the spirit of Will Kent's wife?"

Rap!

"His first wife?"

Rap Rap!

"His second wife, Frances?"

Rap!

"We wish to know how you died, Frances. Did you die naturally?"

Rap! Rap!

"Then, were you murdered?"

Rap!

"Who murdered you, Frances? Was it your husband Will Kent here?"

RAP!

There was a louder clatter as Kent jumped to his feet and the chair crashed to the floor. "You lie, spirit! You lie!

I know I didn't kill my Frances. That's the truth," he roared.

The doctor put a hand on his shoulder to calm him. Kent tore it away. He pointed a thick finger at Parsons. "This ghost must repeat the accusation in front of a magistrate. If it doesn't then you'll suffer for this, Parsons."

"It's not *my* fault," the thin man cringed. "The spirit –"

"It is *your* spirit! You are doing this to get me hanged for killing my wife. The way I see it, Parsons, you are trying to kill me. You are the murderer. And the penalty for attempted murder is death."

"But –" Parsons began to object. Kent and his two friends were already out of the door and pushing through the crowds who had huddled outside to hear the argument.

"We'll just have to prove ourselves in front of a magistrate, Lizzie," the thin man said to his daughter.

"I'll try, Pa," the girl said from her bed. "I'll try."

News of the ghost spread through the streets of London. Crowds gathered at Cock Lane the next day to get a glimpse of the spirit. In the local tavern the landlord Franzen served beer to the crowds. The beer was dearer than usual, but they got their money's worth. "A thin, pale ghost it was. Saw her with my own eyes. Wandering past the window of the house. Wailing and crying."

"When was that, landlord?" someone asked.

"That would be Christmas 1759," Franzen said.

"Then you can't have seen the ghost of Mrs Kent – she didn't die till the February of 1760," the man argued.

The landlord gave a wide, smug smile that showed the blackened stumps of rotting teeth. "Ahh . . . but the *first* Mrs Kent died two years before that."

The crowd gathered closer round the beer barrel. "You

mean he murdered *her* as well?"

The landlord narrowed his red-rimmed eyes. "Arsenic poison in her beer, same as the second Mrs Kent," he said.

"You think the spirit will speak to the magistrate?" someone asked.

"It has to," Franzen said. "It has to."

And a week later Richard Parsons was saying the same thing to little Lizzie. "It has to appear today, Lizzie. Do you understand?"

"Yes, Pa," she said, and there was a tremble of fear in her voice.

"The magistrate will be here in a minute. Are you comfortable?"

"Yes, Pa."

"Good. Then I'll let them into the room. That spirit has to appear today or I'm in trouble, understand?"

"Yes, Pa," the girl murmured and gripped something under the bedclothes.

"Come in, gentlemen," Richard Parsons said. He was twisting a handkerchief in his thin hands.

The magistrate looked at him severely. "You know, Parsons, that it is a serious offence to accuse a man of murder?"

"Oh, yes, your honour. But I'm not accusing anyone. It's the spirit."

"We'll see," Will Kent said as he stepped into the room behind the magistrate.

The two men sat down while Richard Parsons turned towards the bed. "Spirit, are you there?"

This time there was no delay. There was a sharp rap. It seemed to come from the floor under the bed. Will Kent leaned forward. This wasn't the same strange sound that came from the walls before. "Are you the spirit of Frances Kent?" Parsons asked.

Rap!

Kent edged forward again. "Were you murdered, Frances?" Parsons was asking.

Rap!

Will Kent jumped to his feet and snatched the cover off the bed. Lizzie Parsons was lying there in a grubby white night-dress on even grubbier sheets. The big man picked her up easily and dragged her towards the magistrates' chair.

"Show the gentleman what you have in your hand, Lizzie," he shouted.

The terrified girl raised her hand. It held a heavy piece of wood. Kent snatched it and waved it under the magistrate's nose. "Your spirit, I think."

"Richard Parsons, you are under arrest," the magistrate said solemnly. "You are charged with conspiring to bring about the death of William Kent. You will appear before a court tomorrow to answer the charges."

Parsons looked at his daughter.

"Sorry, Pa. I thought that's what you wanted," she said miserably.

All the newspapers of the day wrote about the fraud. None of them were interested in exploring the strange, true happenings before the fraud.

Parsons got two years in jail, four sessions locked in a pillory, and a lot of sympathy. Being locked in the pillory could be a cruel punishment; a man had been stoned to death in the same pillory by angry crowds. When Parsons appeared in the pillory the crowd collected money for him!

It seems some people are determined to believe in ghosts even when fakes have been uncovered. The Cock Lane Ghost was the first time a ghost story had been properly investigated in England.

Would you be able to tell the difference between a real ghost and a fraud if you had the chance? Over the years ghost hunters have drawn up a series of "rules" to try to help people make sensible decisions about ghosts . . .

Ghost Hunting – FACT FILE

Good ghost-hunters will attempt to prove a ghost exists by taking some sort of recording equipment, and will go to the site of a reported haunting prepared for anything.

Ghost-hunting Equipment

Ghost hunters will equip themselves with the following:

- Recording equipment (see ghost-hunting rules)
- Torches (plus spare bulbs and batteries)
- Candles (to test for draughts)
- Thermometer (to check if that chill running down the spine is just fear)
- Compass (to check the direction of a sighting or to sense magnetic change in the site)
- Warm and waterproof clothing
- Food and drink
- Notebook and pens/pencils (to record experiences while they're fresh in the mind)
- Talcum powder (scattered on the floor to test for footprints. Sugar has the same effect but also gives a "crunching" sound to warn of unexpected movement.)
- Thread (stretched across corridors or stairs to catch people who are trying to

fake a ghostly appearance)
- Maps and plans of a place are helpful, especially if they show underground streams and mine tunnels or buried power cables

Ghost hunters can prepare by taking the right equipment. But they also need to follow certain rules if they are going to increase their chances of proving ghosts exist.

Ghost-hunting Rules
1 Hunt in pairs
You may be told that a headless horseman haunts a wood. You go to the wood *expecting to see a headless horseman.* Your imagination *tells* you there is a headless horseman on that path ahead of you. You really believe you see it! A good ghost-hunter will take at least one other person. That second person should know as little as possible about the reports so that they *do not know what to expect.*

2 Take recording equipment
A ghost-hunter is looking for *proof.* The more records you have the better. These records can be
- photographs
- video or film
- tape-recorded sound
- footprints
- temperature changes

3 Be patient

Ghosts don't appear very often or very regularly. If you don't see anything in a graveyard on a particular night then you may have been there on the wrong night. Ghost-hunters often have to try over and over again; they don't give up easily.

4 Look for sensible explanations first

Most ghost reports are simple mistakes: strange knocking sounds that turn out to be central heating pipes; pale phantoms that are simply wisps of fog; eerie lights that are reflections of moonlight on a window. The majority of ghost reports are the result of mistakes.

5 Know the haunt

If you are going to spend a night in a castle then spend as much time as possible getting to know it in the daytime. Ghost-hunters should be able to find their way around even on the darkest nights.

6 Believe no one

Don't believe any report until you have checked it for yourself. People who report the ghost to you could be wrong. They could even be lying. In the history of ghost reports there are a lot of fakers, frauds and liars.

7 Know the history of the place

Try to find out as much about the site of the haunting as possible. You need to find out what was there *before* the building existed. Old maps and local history books from the nearest library might help. Then you need to know as much as possible about the people who used to live in the building. Lastly, you need to talk to people who've lived in the area for a long time; what have they heard or seen?

8 Don't be frightened

That's easy to say, of course! But you have to remember that ghosts rarely harm anyone. There are reports of damage to furniture and to rooms but not to people.

9 Don't move

If something appears then don't move until it disappears, making a note of exactly how it vanishes. Is it through a wall? Try to move to the other side of the wall to see if it appears there. Does it go through a door? Then follow it.

10 Don't speak

Ghosts don't usually talk. It seems as if they move in a world of their own and can't see us. But talking can disturb the conditions and cause them to disappear.

EPILOGUE

Do you believe in ghosts?

When someone asks you that perhaps the best answer is to reply, "What sort of ghosts?" There have been several types described in this book. Some are more likely than others to be true.

Did you know . . .
Most ghosts are not *seen*, but people report
- a sound
- a smell
- a feeling of heat or cold
- a feeling of terror
- mysterious movement of objects
- strange lights or shadows

Ghosts are not something you should worry about. Most "ghostly" experiences turn out to have a natural explanation. (In fact some ghost-hunters reckon that out of every 100 reports only two turn out to be truly unexplained.)

You've read some of the millions of ghost stories that people have told about ghosts. Now do you believe in ghosts?

Only *you* can answer that.